Fifty Good Men and True

THERE'S A VACANT PLACE FOR YOU MY LAD!

YOUR KING AND COUNTRY NEED YOU

To my good friend, Lloyd.
My very best wishes.

Michael Kendrick *Michael Kendrick*

Published by Michael Kendrick
© Michael Kendrick 2005

FORWARD

I was born at Hugglescote in the county of Leicestershire during the late autumn of 1946. The subsequent winter was bitterly cold, the cruellest of the century and offered no sympathy to the immediate post-war Great Britain! My impressionable early years revolved around my parents, and those of my maternal grandparents within their cosy terraced-cottage. By the age of three I was aware that my kinfolk had witnessed major catastrophes, huge losses of life and almost unbearable amounts of suffering! In the cottage, sitting in privileged positions were photographs of grandfather, father, mother and uncle, and all were dressed in military attire.

Lots of books provide information on these two major catastrophes, namely the Great War and World War Two, however, this book specialises on a unique band of young men. Readers of the 1914-18 War may recall the 'Pals' Battalions, being solely comprised of soldiers from a town or city, hence most were pals. My book relates to the same period and concerns just fifty soldiers, all from Coalville and district of northwest Leicestershire. A combination of circumstances meant they were the first civilian volunteers, (or among the very first) to arrive in France to support the depleted British Expeditionary Force. The same applies regarding entry into trench-warfare near to Armentieres. The 'First Fifty,' as they were originally known were all God-fearing lads - the youngest was sixteen! For over half a century their fame lived on as the 'Famous Fifty.' This book is my humble attempt to ensure that their bravery and sacrifice is never forgotten.

Research has been start-stop for almost twenty-years, including many trips to the battlefields. I must confess to adding one or two names to reach the full fifty. They were not randomly taken and vital pointers indicate that it would be an injustice to omit their names. I do hope you find my book worthy of the 'band of pals' described within the following pages.

I firmly believe most aspects of life contain a blend of good and evil, and although I would never condone the savagery of warfare, it does exemplify the spiritual qualities of brotherhood, bravery and sacrifice of young men 'doing what they believed to be right.'

Michael Kendrick.
2004

DEDICATION AND THANKS

With the blessing of my family and friends
I dedicate this book to my dear grandfather,

Charles Hatter.

Only his inspirational memories ensured the book came to fruition.
I thank my dear wife, Beryl, for her love and understanding.
My busy sister, Pamela, for spending hours proofreading.
Denis Baker, an old friend who helped with research.
Martin Bird for his friendship and technical ability.
The Coalville Times for their archival records.
To all contributors mentioned.

Michael Kendrick.

PREFACE BY MAJOR PETER MOORE M.C.

It gave me great pleasure to hear that there was to be a book about the Famous Fifty. It is not difficult to imagine how extremely demanding it must have been for those young men to leave the comforts of civilian life, and to find themselves so rapidly in the company of hardened, trained soldiers in a territorial battalion. What a challenge for these civilians to have to reach the high level of physical fitness demanded, and to adapt themselves to the rigours of army life! I am naturally proud of my father, Captain Aubrey Moore M.C., and of his contribution towards the efforts of the Fifth Battalion of the Leicestershire Regiment. He, in turn, had nothing but praise for those early volunteers. Indeed, he was one of them himself and went to school with at least three of the Fifty. Several served with him in the 'Tunnelling Party' with great bravery and distinction. When he could be persuaded to talk about his Great War experiences, it was clear that, like all good officers, my father had profound respect, admiration and affection for the men he was privileged to command. For this reason he found it a distressing ordeal writing to the next of kin when one of his men was killed. He was a very modest man, and he would have been greatly moved by the warm accounts written within this book about him as an officer and as a man.

For myself, I served with the 2/5th Battalion of the Leicesters in World War Two and I can identify with some of the suffering of the earlier generation. In broad terms, ours was a mobile war, theirs a static war. The static parts were always the worst because one was a sitting target day after day, even month after month in World War One. My own worst memories of World War Two are of when we were stuck for relatively prolonged periods in a defensive position, a sitting target for accurate mortaring and shelling. At such times I comforted myself by the example of fortitude set by my forbears in World War One, when their ordeal was almost certainly far worse.

Having read this well researched and absorbing account, I am grateful that Michael Kendrick has brought to vivid life for us the bravery of the Leicestershire men, who volunteered to fight for their country, many of whom gave their lives for their country in World War One. They were indeed fifty good men and true, famously so. Their story is typical of the magnificent qualities of the fighting men of the First War generation.

We owe a great debt of gratitude to Michael Kendrick for producing this moving testimonial to those brave soldiers, and for ensuring with the publication of this book, that their sacrifices and achievements have been recognised and recorded for posterity.

Many thanks to Peter, whose Leicestershire ancestors include the Moores of Appleby Magna and the Byron family, who has also written his own account of World War Two entitled: 'No Need to Worry.'

Author.

A WALK IN THEIR FOOTPRINTS

My dear wife, Beryl, and I spent half a dozen summer holidays walking in the footprints of the 'Famous Fifty' in France and Flanders. My initial motivation sprang from love of my departed grandfather, Charles Hatter, and that spurred and drove me on. He was one of those 'pals', and I couldn't forget the shrapnel-like pieces of shell casing that peppered his body. Gradually I met the families of names my grandfather had mentioned during our chats of his wartime experiences.

All of the 'First-Fifty' (their original title) were recruited into the 5th (1/5) Territorial Battalion, which was based at Loughborough, and part of the Leicestershire Regiment. The full Battalion comprised of Companies that were located throughout the county. As the war developed several of the Fifty were reposted following promotion to officer rank, or after recovery from wounds, invariably to other Tiger Battalions. I sometimes mention the 4th (1/4th) Leicestershire Battalion, a sister battalion that recruited from the city of Leicester, and which followed the same pathway throughout the war.

The Great War or World War 1 as it became known erupted with shock waves of volcanic force on the 4th August 1914. The history books point to the assassination of Archduke Franz Ferdinand and his wife, Duchess Sophie, as the underlying hotbed for the conflagration. Yes, he was heir to the Habsburg throne but his death was little more than a final strike-of-a-match to an existing powder keg of virulent nationalism. In Europe, Great Britain and France held the senior political and influential positions, and they appeared particularly secure thanks to earlier colonial expansion. Their colonies brought in a mass of raw material, expanded trade links and above all created worldwide prestige. Germany on the other hand only became a nation in 1871, and in general terms was too late to follow the golden trail. The deadly sin of envy was the primary cause of the first planetary war, with Germany considering their predicament unjust as they struggled to build a colonial empire, especially in Africa. Tensions soared to the point whereby the fatherland decided to flex its military muscle, with lethal and devastating consequences. Austria-Hungary's ancient polyglot empire had become sullen as minorities pushed for change, and a fanned-air of destabilisation existed. Leaders also felt worried and insecure about the growing Russian strength challenging her Balkan policy. Indeed Russia was looking to a war as a safety valve to relieve pent-up emotions relating to ambitions and frustrations within her internal make-up.

The Great War of 1914-18 shook monarchs from their thrones, destroyed four empires, and severely damaged the social fabric of life on a worldwide scale. The cost in human life was twelve-and-a-half million, although some estimates are way above this figure, additionally thirty-seven and a half million were wounded, taken prisoner of war or missing. The total economic cost of the war £75,077,000,000. I present these as cold statistics, but every figure resulted in heartbreak for huge chunks of society in the 'civilised' world.

On the 2nd August 1914, the men of the 4th and 5th Leicestershire Battalions marched into their Bank Holiday training camp at the seaside resort of Bridlington, on England's east coast. A portentous downpour of rain, thunder and lightning signalled their arrival, and soon they were under bell-top canvas and within sight of the North Sea. On that very same day heavy black-clouds of war loomed over Europe, as Kaiser Wilhelm 11, Emperor of Germany and King of Prussia, demanded that Belgium allow free access for German troops to invade France. At daybreak the

For September and October 1914 the First Fifty encamped on a field in Charnwood Forest, which pre-war soldiers of the 5th Leicestershire Battalion often used for training purposes. Now reverted to agricultural land, the pines and deciduous trees that are a backdrop were also part of the training area, so too the tors of granite rock just beyond them.

The tors were familiar to the First Fifty. Often they stood on top of these ancient granite incisors to look down upon the agriculturally fertile and coal-rich plains below. In 1914 it was easily possible to discern the town of Coalville and the various villages such as Hugglescote and Whitwick.

Thringstone House today, ninety years earlier it was the village institute and used by the First Fifty for training purposes, several days a week. The frontage is an old farmhouse that was bought by Charles and Mary Booth, the famous Victorian benefactors and social scientists. The pair investigated the social conditions of the English lower classes at a critical moment in the history of social reform and lived nearby at Grace Dieu Manor House.

following morning, amid an atmosphere of tension the Leicestershire Battalions received orders to immediately return to the Magazine at Leicester, and the barracks at Loughborough respectively. The 4th arrived by half past eight in the evening; insufficient transport meant that the 5th arrived at two-thirty the following morning. On August 4th it was announced that the Regular Army and all Reservists were in a state of mobilisation. The military was on a war footing.

On that summer's day soldiers of the Territorial Force could be seen drilling and engaging in other military practices on the parks of Loughborough and Leicester's Western Park (about one mile from the city centre).

In Loughborough, local civilians cancelled their holidays and men in khaki could be seen almost everywhere throughout the town. Shortly they entrained for Duffield in Derbyshire, with an opportunity to reorganise and to discuss adjustments regarding responsibilities of duty. The Territorial Force was founded in 1908, the aim to attract men keen on the ideal of military service, but for whatever reason (age or profession) limited by circumstances to defend the homeland only.

On August 13th at Duffield a proposition was put to the 5th Battalion to fight abroad, and they answered in a very positive manner, over ninety per-cent declaring availability for frontline service, whether at home or abroad. Those willing agreed to sign the necessary form of acceptance at a later date. On August 15th they entrained from Derby Station with a destination of Luton. The Bedfordshire town was becoming chock-a-block with territorial soldiers (terriers) and they were billeted wherever possible, mostly in schools. The 5th secured Beech Hill School until October 2nd, when they took-up lodgings in West Luton, with the name of Station Road often being mentioned. The Battalion headquarters and officers' billet was Ceylon Hall, a Baptist Chapel, and it was there that the men 'signed-on' for service overseas, thus over-riding earlier contracts relating to Home defence only.

The 4th and 5th Leicestershire Battalions originally formed part of The Lincolnshire and Leicestershire Brigade, but on the 12th May 1915 became the 138th Brigade of the 46th North Midland Division. General

Some of the Fifty with relatives and friends ready to entrain for barracks. August 1914.

two miles from Coalville's town centre at a place called High Tor in the Charnwood Forest. The Leicestershire Regiment had used this field several times beforehand, and placing the Fifty under canvas was considered part of the toughening-up process. Occasions arose when they were billeted in Coalville, especially prior to church services. There was an officer in charge, and a Sergeant Stone of the Seaforth Highlanders instilled some military discipline and basic training. Nearby Thringstone Institute was also used for this purpose. High Tor offers excellent views over the Coalville plain, and one can imagine the thoughts of the Fifty as they sat around campfires at night, seeing the twinkling lights of their hometown below.

Possibly one or two were fearful of what they had

Sir Ian Hamilton and the famed Lord Kitchener of Khartoum inspected the Division before it left Luton. The park at Luton Hoo echoed to the strident orders of military command as the Division marched past and paraded thousands of well-built, suntanned, khaki-clad soldiers with bayonets sparkling in the autumn sunshine. Authoritative voices were heard to comment: 'The cream of manhood from the Midlands.'

A few days later King George V inspected them, and he too was similarly impressed.

At the outbreak of war a considerable number of city and county men volunteered to join the Forces, and they were more than required as Great Britain's Regular Army was relatively small. The 1914 British Expeditionary Force to France consisted of only one hundred thousand men, and eighty thousand rapidly became casualties.

Fortune, 'or perhaps lack of it' intervened when senior officers in the 5th Battalion selected fifty recruits from Coalville and district, to counter the missing eight percent who vetoed service overseas. The conception was complete and the birth of the 'Famous Fifty' was to follow very shortly.

The 'First Fifty' was selected from late August to early September 1914; it involved medicals and inspection of physical ability, also of personal recommendation. They assembled at Coalville Railway Station for visits to the Drill Hall in Granby Street, Loughborough, and Wigston Barracks near to Leicester. Upon their return they encamped on a field

The First Fifty on the march in civvies, early October 1914.

let themselves in for. Often on a Sunday the Fifty paraded to different places of worship, usually accompanied by a local band, and were acclaimed for their smartness. In the third week of October the Fifty entrained at Coalville East Railway Station for Loughborough Drill Hall where they were kitted-out with uniforms and rifles. A photograph taken at the time shows eleven of them in Leopold Street, close to the town centre. With the group are other territorial soldiers sporting cap badges, the eleven having to wait a while for their 'Tiger'. A few days later they were ordered to pack up their equipment on High Tor and to join the 5th Leicestershire Battalion at Luton to continue a period of intensive training.

Some of the Fifty photographed in Leopold Street, Loughborough.

The Departure

It was on Friday the 30th October 1914, a frosty morning that the fifty fresh-faced lads marched down the hill towards Hugglescote's St John The Baptist Church for a short service. They were joined by the Hugglescote and Ellistown Brass Band, and marched along Central Road (then known as North Street) and paused to have their photograph taken at the rear of 168, Central Road (where my future grandmother lived). They continued their march along Belvoir Road with the tin whistle and the drums setting the tone, and turned right towards Coalville Midland Railway Station. (Very movingly, every November 11th (Remembrance Day) a service is held by the Clock Tower Memorial and a parade is held along High and Hotel Streets, so following in their footsteps). The Coalville Times newspaper commented on their smartness and: *'The railway station bridge and surrounding approaches were crowded with hundreds of people and the Coalville lads had a most hearty send off.'*

The huge crowd included the Vicar, Curate and many of the leading residents of the town and district. My grandfather's youngest sister, Nellie Hatter, later Moore, told me how she waved to her brother at 'Baxton's Corner', (corner at the junction of Forest Road and Central Road) and followed the procession all the way to the station. *'I was so proud of Charlie, but I could not stop the tears from flowing.'* The same applied to Elsie Hart, later Ramsell, who watched her elder brother Frederick Wilfred Hart.

The Fifty received cigarettes and chocolates and the crowd sang the 1914 hit song: 'It's A Long Way To Tipperary' together with other popular martial airs. The train whistled anxiously, the platform was a sea of hugs and tears, coach doors slammed-to and at 9.00 am massive wheels slowly revolved to announce departure.

The First Fifty in October 1914. Taken at the rear of 168 Central Road in Hugglescote.

Clouds of steam vented into the air and the chuffs complemented the cheers. The crowd continued to cheer as khaki arms continued to wave until the train finally disappeared around the bend a few hundred

A winter's day. Coalville Railway Station (circa 1912). The First Fifty left from here in October 1914 amid large crowds as the train departed. Direction as photograph.

yards on. Over half of the First Fifty would never see the town's High Street again.

The Battalion Diary reported with military brevity: **'Fifty men have been added to our strength.'**

By the end of October 1914 another 120 local men had enlisted as volunteers into other battalions. Army life was undoubtedly tough, most days involved marches of over twenty-five miles. Every day they marched from their billets to the training areas north of Luton, and they strictly followed a schedule - having to be at the 16th milestone on the Bedford road by a given time.

Eventually, as described earlier, the First Fifty marched alongside the cream of the Midland's manhood at Luton Hoo and were saluted by the King.

At 1.00 am on Monday the 16th November 1914 orders were received to prepare for an 8 am move to Ware in Hertfordshire. A wag comically asked, 'Where?' The roads of 1914 dictated a marching distance of twenty-five miles. Vehicles of all kinds were obtained including wagons, milk floats, brewers' drays and their equipment was packed. A variety of horses were requisitioned - too many not up to the task, and on steep hills manpower had to come into its own. A tired wag, the same one was heard to comment, 'This is very wearing.' It must be written that battalion comics (wags) helped enormously to maintain morale, especially in the dark days of France and Flanders. During the route march there was an hourly halt of ten minutes, and when they reached Ware at 7.30 pm they

rested for a day. A little further on they stopped for two nights at the village of Much Hadham and then travelled onwards to Bishops Stortford. Here they were to find an increase in field exercises and middle-of-the-night manoeuvres.

On November 26th they marched to Sawbridgeworth and were billeted there. Training was hard but recreation was available in the form of football, boxing, concerts and the odd dance evening, especially at Christmas, which was spent in the town. A few romances started with some of the local girls with most ending with a partner buried in a foreign field. There was plenty of food and lots of cheer, and a few of the lads had a spell of leave around this time.

At noon on the 25th February 1915 orders were received to entrain at midnight at Harlow Station, and the following morning they arrived at Southampton Docks. Destination France. Half the Battalion embarked aboard the 'SS Duchess of Argyll' and the remainder on the 'SS Atlanta'. Both were old Clyde River steamers and they bravely steamed out at 9.00 pm to an accompaniment of ships' sirens blowing a 'farewell.' The weather was atrocious with a howling gale whipping-up treacherous seas. The 'Duchess' somehow crossed safely to Le Havre, arriving in the early hours of the 26th February 1915, but the other had to turn back and depart a day later, still in terrible

5th Leicestershire Battalion on the march at Luton.

conditions to arrive at daybreak. My grandfather (on the Duchess) told me that all of the troops were violently seasick and everyone feared for their life aboard the ramshackle boat amid the tempestuous Channel waves. They received quite a buffeting and as each wave crashed into them they thought it was an enemy torpedo. The 5th Battalion began the landings

Cap badge of the Leicestershire Regiment.

The regular British Army had fought so valiantly against overwhelming German forces, and the survivors were reassured to see reinforcements, and passed-on their experiences and know-how to the relatively raw troops. The British Expeditionary Force (B.E.F.), close on one hundred thousand soldiers, crossed the Channel between the 12th and 20th August 1914 to support the French Army. The B.E.F. advanced and laid out their stall in the little Belgium mining-town of Mons. Labelled: 'That Contemptible Little Army' by the German Kaiser, because they were so heavily outnumbered by German Forces, they did exceptionally well until withdrawing to avoid being cut off due to problems with nearby French Forces. So began the long retreat and escalating casualties, and in spite of the Germans receiving a serious setback in the September Battle of the Marne, a stalemate subsequently set in.

of the 46th North Midland Division, correctly carrying the boast: 'The first full Territorial Division to arrive in France.' A few territorial battalions landed independently before them but I cannot find any information to contradict that the **First Fifty were the first of the August 1914 volunteers to set foot in France.** I would like the good folk of Leicestershire to always remember this. The dreadful weather persisted and our 4th Battalion crossed the Channel one week later. Very soon both battalions saw active service in the trenches.

Cartoon of The Kaiser sketched on the reverse of a Christmas card, sent from the trenches.

The Germans dug deep, complex defensive trench systems, a 'what we have we hold' philosophy, whilst initially the Allies dug crude trenches to prevent any further loss of ground, but with an onus always on attack. The area between the trenches was simply called 'No-Man's Land' and the total massive earthwork was named: 'The Western Front'. It stretched from the Swiss border to the North Sea, a length of 736 kilometres (460 miles). The depth of the trench was determined by the water table. Where the reading was high the trenches were of necessity shallower, and so parapets had to be constructed to form 'high command' trenches. Soft digging in the Ypres area meant that trenches needed careful revetting to stop a cave-in, whereas digging on the Somme's chalky soil was harder but the finished article was more robust. Both sides also laid barbed wire hedging in front of their trenches, it was very strong and thick and, unless hit and dispersed by high-explosive shells, was impenetrable to man.

The village of Hardifort in France. The 5th Leicestershire billeted in the barns in March 1915.

Life in the trenches

The First Fifty fought on the Western Front. For some it was their 'home' for the best part of four years. To appreciate this environment, consider how tough it would be for most of us to live in a hole in the ground. Add to this a multitude of large rats that bite whilst you are asleep (in prime form from consuming so much flesh), and being constantly riddled with fleas. Also, water and food would often be rationed, you'd bake in summer's hot sun, and during storms have to wade waist-deep in the foulest of water. Remember to boil this water for some of your drinks.

A soldier peers cautiously over the edge of the trench while others sleep.

Further to this, soldiers slept in holes (dug-outs) in the trenches in all weathers including snow and frost, and the enemy killed them with shellfire, trench mortars, sniping, trench raids and gas-attacks. Health wise the conditions were ripe for bronchial-pneumonia, dysentery, gangrenous sores and trenchfoot (skin and flesh rots when feet are immersed in water for too long), frostbite and trench fever (akin to influenza).

The 5th Leicestershire disembarked at Le Havre early on the 27th and 28th February 1915. They received an issue of sheepskin coats and extra socks and marched to the railway station where they entrained in wagons, 'Hommes 36-40, Chevaux en long 8'. They were roasting hot in the summer and frost-cold in winter and provided no sanitation. The Battalion departed at 7.00 pm and arrived the following afternoon at Arneke Station at 2.35 pm. There followed an eight kilometre (five miles) march in snow-blizzards to the village of Hardifort, where they enjoyed

a break of three days. Here they shaved and smartened themselves but found winter barn life bitterly cold, in spite of ample quantities of freshly laid straw.

In early March 1915 the 5th Leicestershire (including the First Fifty) experienced twenty-four hours in frontline trenches at Le Bizet, a mile to the north of Armentieres. **Only four months earlier the First Fifty were in civilian attire, and if not the first volunteers they were among the very first to witness trench life.** They were accompanied by regular troops of the Essex and Lancashire Fusiliers who taught them the basics of survival. The death of Shepshed's 2nd Lieutenant G. Aked by a sniper focussed minds and they learned quickly.

Spanbroekmolen stands at the centre and rear. Tens of thousands of soldiers died on these fields.

On April 1st they moved the short distance to a sector known as the Messines Ridge, an area where months earlier British and French troops were engaged in fierce battles against the Germans. Remnants of battle were evident with decaying bodies of both human and animal; and when possible our lads buried them. This was an unavoidable task that any person would find almost unbearable. In early 1915 the Messines' trenches were only a few feet deep and lives were lost because of this, and also whilst attempting to deepen them. **Several of the First Fifty perished here.** Around this time they had their first acquaintance with gas, the Germans introducing it as their new weapon only four miles to the north at Ypres. Soldiers were seen walking in single file, coughing, wheezing, eyes weeping and blind, trying to support one another. A fearful sight and a dire warning to inescapable events for future battles.

Spanbroekmolen Hill on the Messines Ridge. Several of The Fifty were killed on this field in 1915. The top of the hill was blown off by a mine in 1917.

sniper fire could be heard. In this concealing darkness a new trench-line needed to be dug, and the War Diary states: *'All digging records were broken as a consequence of enemy fire.'* The location, ironically so, was close to a lethal position - the ruins of Zillebeke Church. Here, **another of the Fifty fell** to ground with spirit spent. As the first rays of dawn appeared over the killing fields the depth of digging was to a suitable standard. Several salvoes of enemy shells 'encouraged' the Battalion to rapidly retire along the embankment, and buses returned them to the Messines Sector. It was at this time that the Division suffered the first terrifying roar and quake-tremors of mining. The enemy dug a vertical shaft, tunnelled under their trenches, planted explosives and detonated to maximum effect. The Battalion's commanding officer, Lieutenant Colonel C. H. Jones, appointed Lieutenant Aubrey Moore (a mining engineer in civilian life) to select soldiers with a mining background to counter this latest enemy initiative. The area was close to Hill 76 (Spanbroekmolen) and our forward trenches were only forty yards from the enemy line. Lieutenant Moore and forty-nine men undertook the duty of sappers, an extremely dangerous occupation. Soon a gallery was dug deep below ground, and Lieutenant Moore, upon hearing German excavations immediately laid some ammonal and destroyed their efforts. Such operations were called 'defensive or counter mining' and they resulted in the saving of many British lives. A collection of four medals, three Distinguished Conduct Medals, (D.C.M.) and one Military Cross (M.C.) illustrates the quality and bravery of this honourable team, which included several of the Fifty.

To all troops the very name of Ypres was fearsome and synonymous with both suffering and death. Its infamous reputation resulted from both sides suffering appalling casualties earlier in the war. Because it was a salient (bulge) into the enemy line, it resulted in a concentration of firepower from three directions.

The power of enemy shelling was notoriously accurate and huge chunks of historical and beautiful Ypres lay in ruins. The 14th May 1915 brought an evening's work for the 5th Battalion, and their toils

The 46th Division was requested to pass on knowledge and trench experiences to elite troops from British regiments recently arrived in France. Unfortunately, many considered it beneath them to receive advice from 'mere territorial soldiers' and as a result large numbers were killed, mostly being sniped over the parapet. On the night of June 16th the

were in nightmarish conditions within the Salient. Following a trek in the inky blackness they saw the Cloth Tower and other buildings smouldering with a dull red glow. One part of the pathway took them along a railway embankment (see photograph), and

The railway embankment near to Ypres. The 5th Leicestershire used this often as they travelled up to Zillebeke and Sanctuary Wood for trenches 35 and 50.

Battalion left the trenches and marched to some huts at Locre for what the War Diary describes as: *'A very pleasant five days rest.'*

On the night of the 29th June 1915 the 5th marched to the outskirts of Ypres, crossed 'Shrapnel Corner' and eventually reached the northern edge of Zillebeke Lake. On the western edge was a twenty feet bank, and within this, which acted as cover from small arms fire, the Lake Dug-outs, their home whilst a support battalion. At dusk they travelled with caution

The church at Zillebeke. An unpleasant locality! One of the Fifty died near here.

to Zillebeke, past the ruins of the village church and around the iniquitous 'Hill 60'. For thousands of soldiers this carbuncle of a man-made hill was to be their last vision on earth. Perhaps, metre-by-metre it was the most heinous place on the Western Front. They continued on an eastern route to Sanctuary Wood, and along to take over frontline trenches 49, 50 and support trench 51. The German frontline was a mere two hundred and sixty metres away (two hundred

yards) and the sniping was known to be lethal. A later tour of duty took them to Trench 35 (Bomb Corner) where they were closer at 90 metres, and where enemy mines had damaged trenches 36 and 37 just twenty-four hours before they accommodated them.

Whilst the Battalion was in Trench 50, and just after posting night sentries on the evening of July 23rd the Germans detonated a large mine beneath them, resulting in deaths and many casualties. The situation would have been far worse but for the bravery of the sappers who dismantled another mine a week later, shortly before it was due to explode.

On the night of July 30th the 5th Battalion was shelled at Maple Copse, at a cost of thirty-five casualties.

The Ypres Salient continued to reap the lives of the young soldiers from Leicestershire, and many of them can be found at rest in Sanctuary Wood cemetery.

The 5th was more than pleased to hand over their frontline trenches to the Wiltshire Regiment on October 1st. During an eight-week period in Trench 50 many lives were lost including **six of the Fifty**, and **another** one in Trench 35.

Maple Copse Cemetery near Zillebeke. *'In a short time we had 23 casualties from shellfire.'* (Captain J. D. Hills, 5th Leicestershire Battalion).

The next posting was very much a case of 'out of the frying pan and into the fire'. The 25th September 1915 is marked as a black day in many British Regimental War Diaries: the first day of the Battle of Loos. Bravery was a hallmark, but such qualities count for little when troops are exhausted from long route marches and lack of sleep, and then thrown to the power of German weaponry. Like too many battles of the Great War it dragged on for what seemed an eternity, neither side knowing when to cut losses proportionate to possible gains. Qualifying this instance the 4th and 5th Battalions fought side-by-side

The troops were sent to Marseilles to await embarkation.
They thought they were in heaven!

During their return journey the train was stopped at Paris because of a German air raid. Our lads had the surreal experience of German and French aeroplanes dog-fighting in a night-sky illuminated by searchlights. The French aeroplanes had small searchlights attached and so their climbing and diving could be monitored. Anti-aircraft guns fired shells which exploded with sudden flashes and roars in the sky, and bombs thundered on impact with buildings, and so created fires.

on October 13th at the Hohenzollern Redoubt, just to the north of Loos. The resulting loss of life was horrendous and I have written of this battle later in the book, so too with Trench 50.

The Battalions regrouped in billets close to the Nieppe Forest, and had their depleted numbers increased with fresh officers and troops from England. The 4th in particular was badly hit with losses of twenty officers and 453 other ranks. As a partial remedy to aid regrouping, Major Toller (a Quorndon man) of the 5th was placed in command of the 4th Battalion.

Shortly matters and location improved, the War Diary states: *From a bloody war, it became not a good war but a lovely war.* On the 6th January 1916 they marched to Berguette Station and boarded a trainload of cattle trucks destined for Marseilles, southern France, and the Mediterranean. The troops couldn't believe what was happening to them - from the mud of Flanders to the cleansing blue of a semi-tropical sea. On January 20th they embarked on 'H.M.T. Andania', a Cunard liner and the height of luxury. For two days the men thought they were in heaven, however on the 22nd they disembarked and entrained for a return to the quagmires of France. There had been talk of a posting to the Dardanelles or Egypt, but it was all cut-short by Lord Kitchener after he visited the Dardanelles and said, *'Enough is enough, everybody out.'* His decision certainly extended the lives of many a Leicestershire lad.

The Battalion's next posting was in the Neuville St. Vaast - Souchez Sector, more familiarly known as Vimy Ridge. They relieved French troops on the 9th March 1916. Earlier, in May of 1915 the French attacked strongly at Vimy and drove the Germans off the heights, but the enemy managed to retain the Ridge. In September of 1915 another terrific battle saw the opposing armies sharing the Ridge with frontlines barely thirty-five metres apart. Following a heroic battle by the Zouaves in the steep-sided valley, 'Talus de Zouaves', the amount of corpses and smell was appalling, and it was in this valley where the Battalion's dugouts were located.

Part of the trench system used by the 5th Leicestershire Battalion at Vimy Ridge.
Two of the Fifty died here.

The shelling and sniping was as bad as Ypres, the trenches were bitterly cold and many lads suffered from Trench Foot. The Germans were particularly fond of what was called the 'minenwerfer'. It was virtually a five-gallon oil drum (about twenty-two litres) filled with explosives and fired by a piece of fuse, lit at the point of launch. It was a terrible blow to the 5th Battalion when such a weapon killed Captain Roland Farmer ('C' Company), of Ashby de la Zouch. He was described as the bravest officer of his time, a man well liked by all and his body was found head down in a water-filled shell hole. Mining and shelling was heavy and prevalent in this sector, and **two of the Fifty** died at this desolate spot.

Looking down the Zouave Valley towards Souchez. The 5th Battalion called it 'The valley of the dead'.

After night sentries were posted, small groups of men would sit around a brazier and mash a cup of tea before retiring to a cold 'fox-hole' for some sleep.

With a mist creeping along deep trenches and with a firelight glow on their faces, they would chat and sing classics such as Ivor Novello's, 'Keep the Home Fires Burning.'

'Keep the home fires burning,
While your hearts are yearning,
Though your lads are far away
they dream of home,
There's a silver lining,
Through the dark world shining,
Turn the dark cloud inside out,
Till the boys come home.'

(Unfortunately, nearly one million of our boys didn't come home.)

On the 8th May 1916 the Battalions were transported to Mont St. Eloi where they spent a night under canvas. The hill was (and still is) clearly visible for miles around and the view of the battlefields on the plain below spectacular. This was not the case regarding their location on the slopes of Vimy Ridge, whereby the German Forces held a panoramic view of Lens and the surrounding hinterland.

May 10th signalled the start of a very pleasant ten days stay in the quaint old village of Lucheux, which adjoins ancient forestland, and is thirty-two kilometres (twenty miles) northwest of Albert on the Somme. It was a chance for rest, light training and musketry practice. The lads enthused about the warmer weather,

The 5th Leicestershire Batallion football team, 1916. Second row from front on the right is Charles Hatter, third row extreme left Sgt. Walter Butterworth, third row, 4th from the right is Lawrence Gough.

good billets, improved food and the opportunity to write several letters to loved ones at home. Also, the 4th's and the 5th's football teams played their way through to a Brigade final. There were just two minutes remaining and the score stood at 2-2, when the large crowd saw the 4th score a late goal to win 3-2 amid much revelry.

My grandfather was playing for the 5th and he and the rest of the side were none too pleased when they conceded such a late goal.

After ten days at Lucheux they moved closer to the frontline and were billeted in barns at the village of Souastre. From this base they frequently travelled to the village of Foncquevillers, which was opposite to the enemy citadel of Gommecourt, to repair and strengthen the sides of the trenches. Meanwhile preparations were ongoing for the whole Division to be involved in an attack against Gommecourt, which stood on the northern edge of the Somme Sector in France. A full-sized model of the German trench system to be attacked was dug near to Lucheux, and rehearsing the campaign tactics was regular and comprehensive. (Probably too much so).

The main street, Souastre, near Gommecourt. 'In the large barns the 'Bow Bells' performed a large variety of songs and sketches. Many a soldier welcomed these evening entertainments and remembered them for years afterwards.'

During the nineteen-thirties and onwards the veterans, usually over a drink, relived their warm memories of evenings at Souastre. In the large barns the 'Bow Bells' performed nightly for the soldiers. These morale-boosting, wonderfully pleasurable interludes of songs and sketches 'the drummer-ballet-dancer', and such melodies as, 'O Roger Rum' were never forgotten by the old campaigners.

June of 1916 could not have been wetter and conditions in the trenches suffered as a result, full of water and sides collapsing, so the opening day of the Battle of the Somme had to be postponed until July 1st. The plan for the attack was to capture the German fortified villages from Serre in the north to Montauban in the south, and to puncture a way through with an advance to Bapaume. All of this was to be achieved within a few days.

The battle-experienced 46th North Midland Territorial Division's attack was to be used as a decoy. Measures were taken to give the Germans the impression that the main thrust of the British attack would be at Gommecourt, just to the north of Serre. In early June, the German commander at Gommecourt reported to Prince Rupprecht of an increase in British Forces, and the 2nd Guard Reserve Division was sent to strengthen the citadel.

All along the Line our artillery pounded the German front and communication trenches for a week, until finally at 6.40 am on July 1st they opened up yet again, and with even greater intensity. It was a gorgeous summer's morning in Picardy, warm and sunny.

At 7.30 am a smoke screen was laid and four waves of infantry went 'over the top' and crossed into No-Man's-Land. These were men of the 5th and 7th Sherwood Foresters on the left, and two Staffordshire Battalions, the 5th and 6th on the right. The Devil himself must have stirred the light breeze that blew the smoke away, to expose our valiant young men to murderous machine-gun fire. Shrapnel shells joined in the melee; they exploded directly above our forlorn khaki clad figures for a horrific scene too severe for hell. As planned, Captain Ward Jackson and Company Sergeant Major J. R. Hill (of Coalville) led two platoons from the 5th Leicestershire to a point in No-Man's-Land known as the Sucrerie. The scheme was to rapidly dig a trench for a manoeuvrable tactical advantage, and in spite of terrific fire they succeeded in digging a shallow one. However, the enemy concentrated their full fire upon them and Captain Jackson was badly wounded, others also, and they had to retire to their frontlines. The heroic sergeant major (later D.C.M.) saved his captain's life by carrying him from the carnage that was around. The rest of the Battalion was in trenches waiting for the order to attack

when enemy shells dropped all round, and an officer and sergeant major were killed. The scene was pitiful. The chatter of machine-guns, the screaming and explosion of shells, the dead and dying in No-Man's-Land, and tangled and mutilated bodies in our trenches. I was told that the volume of cacophonous sound was so brain numbing that it was almost impossible to think. The troops were superbly trained, but when the flow of the battle did not match its intended course then confusion reigned. The Divisional attack was halted. During the night, parties from the 5th and others helped to rescue some of the wounded that lay on the battleground, with Captain Barton displaying immense bravery saving several lives. Many authoritative accounts have been written on the Battle of the Somme, especially the failings of the opening day. Firstly, the inadequacy of the week-long allied barrage, crucially failing to destroy the strategically placed barbed wire in front of the German lines. Too many shells failed to explode, and insufficient numbers of high-explosive (H.E.) shells were used. (The only effective weapon against such stout wiring). Secondly, the German defensive bunkers were also much deeper than anticipated, and also fortified with reinforced concrete. After the barrage ceased, the largely unscathed enemy surfaced and reaped a rich harvest with machine-guns.

Gommecourt, where enemy machine-gunners reaped such a random harvest.

I am always moved by the lyrics of the song, 'Roses Of Picardy.' Fred Weatherly wrote it shortly after the Battle, and the heart-warming music is by Hayden Wood:

> 'Roses are shining in Picardy,
>
> in the hush of the silvery dew,
>
> Roses are flowering in Picardy,
>
> but there's never a rose like you!
>
> And the roses will die with the summertime,
>
> and our roads may be far apart,
>
> But there's one rose that dies not in Picardy,
>
> 'tis the rose that I keep in my heart!'

Likewise, I empathise with the poets who write about the lost flower of a generation. How machine-guns and shells claimed many a rose, mostly in full bloom, always blood-red roses. Perhaps it is a trait of mine being related to Leicestershire's Great War Poet, Lieutenant Arthur Newbury Choyce.

The 1st July 1916 was the blackest day in the history of the British Army with losses of twenty thousand dead and forty thousand wounded, many within the first hour of battle. A large percentage of the latter struggled through their lives with lost limbs and other grotesque injuries. As a boy in the 1950's, I vividly recall old soldiers limping around Coalville; one in particular comes to mind. The veteran had no legs, just a stump of a body propped-up in his usual spot against the wall of a corner public house facing the Memorial Clock Tower. One cold and rainy day grandfather purposely stopped to buy a box of matches, and to chat to the pitiful soul. As we walked away I learned he was an officer in the Great War, that he'd been scarred both physically and mentally. I can recall another occasion, perhaps it was Remembrance Day, when once again he was in the same spot and tears were trickling down his cheeks.

On the 3rd July 1916 the Battalion left Gommecourt, moving a little to the north to take over trenches opposite Monchy-au-Bois, an undulating and fairly open terrain. They occupied this sector for several months, moving between trenches at Bienvillers whilst in support, and further back to Pommiers as Divisional reserve. Activity on both sides was spasmodic, but it was occasionally intense with the worst feature being the use of gas. As mentioned earlier the Germans used it first at Ypres, and we retaliated - although both sides detested its use. Captain Aubrey Moore ('C' Company) wrote of the annoying coding system, for instance, gas was referred to as 'Gertie' and the release of such 'To Tickle', etc. The Captain also wrote about seeing a German aeroplane shooting down a nearby 'spotter balloon.' Both victims bailed-out before the attack but for one the parachute failed to open, the dead man in question was Basil Hallam, a very famous actor of the times.

Once again the weather was so dreadfully wet that the trench pumps could not accommodate the volume of water, and in places it was six feet in depth. I know for certain that the soldiers who endured these conditions were to suffer terribly in later life from rheumatic disorders and premature arthritic problems. The tour (length) of frontline duty was usually four days, but in quieter areas it could be five or six, and relief was usually at night for obvious safety reasons.

Early in September 1916 the 138th Brigade (1/4th and 1/5th Leicestershire and 1/4th and 1/5th of the Lincolnshire Regiment) held a sports meeting for a bit of light relief.

Sniper's mirror used by Charles Hatter.

Towards the end of October an incident provided an anecdote containing a strong proverbial flavour. Opposite to our frontline our snipers, of which grandfather was one, regularly saw an elderly, white-haired German who looked so benign that none had the heart to harm him. For several weeks he dug-away in an innocent if laboured fashion, but an occasion arose when one of our aircraft flew low overhead, and he violently shook his fist and gestured many a curse. One of our snipers brought his life to an abrupt end. (Not my grandfather I hasten to add).

On October 29th they marched to Millencourt for a period of intensive training in preparation for a special offensive. For two or three days physical training and bayonet practise took place, also some night manoeuvres. To finish off the affair another inter-battalion Brigade football competition took place. The 5th Leicestershire defeated the 4th Lincolnshire, but once again lost to their archrivals the 4th Leicestershire, in a very hard fought final, the touchline language was described as more than coarse.

On December 6th the Brigade marched once again to Souastre and its barns before returning to their old Monchy Sector. It was a wet and cold Christmas, and the opening days of 1917 brought heavy snowfalls and continuous frosts until the middle of February 1917. Conditions were bitter and matters didn't improve when drink carriers often fell into frozen shell holes spilling hot drinks for the lads. They were certainly a tough generation and hot drink or not they survived those semi-artic conditions, they had no alternative.

Shortly came a little trip south to take over two kilometres (2,500 yards) of frontline trench in their old posting opposite to Gommecourt. The thaw had set in and most days were shrouded in thick mists, and for several days heavy enemy shelling reduced visibility at times to nil. Several patrols tested the resolution and alertness of the German lines, yet in spite of withdrawals by compatriots in the south of the Somme, they remained obstinate.

Gommecourt had snowfalls in early March, and on the fifth of the month the 5th Battalion attacked with vigour, especially their bombing parties. After first capturing the wood, the area around the church succumbed. The 8th Sherwood Foresters then relieved the 5th Leicestershire Battalion, and they returned to Souastre for a very well earned break.

In the second week of March they marched through the fallen village of Gommecourt, and were saddened to see some of the old residents returning to survey the wreckage - piles of bricks, which once had been their homes. **Two of the Fifty died here.**

Life in the trenches was extremely tough, but the soldiers of the Great War had their moments. As mentioned earlier they had braziers and rations of coke, where gatherings chatted on frosty nights around a cheery glow. As long as they received sufficient water they brewed-up tea, cocoa, etc, and parcels from home added spice to bully beef and biscuits, sometimes the meals were adequate. Occasional supplies of bacon gave the whole trench a completely different and mouth-watering aroma. During bitterly cold days or prior to an attack, a very special liquor was issued and carefully supervised. It was rum; the old soldiers swore by it and regularly relived the pleasures of the warming, alcoholic, medicinal beverage. They used to joke that teetotallers would soon be cured.

On April 16th they travelled to Annezin, just outside of Bethune, and a few days later a posting to the instantly recognisable 'Double Crassier'. This was a long double slagheap near to Loos, which saw such ferocious fighting in September 1915. The Battalion occupied a small salient in front of Cite St. Pierre, and to their displeasure were overlooked and shelled from three directions. The trenches were as dangerous as any that they had to occupy during the entire war, also,

because of heavy enemy shelling and machine-gun fire from infiltrators at night, they were always short of drinking water.

The 12th May 1917 brought some welcome relief after a terrible journey during which they were constantly shelled. They were billeted in Red Mill, a large red-bricked chateau near to Lievin, a suburb of Lens and it stood on the banks of the River Souchez. The weather was fine and warm and a swimming pool was constructed by damming the river. A certain 2nd Lieutenant J. C. Barrett proved to be a strong swimmer, and at a later date he displayed magnificent courage that was recognised by the award of a Victoria Cross. Their trenches lay between the Souchez River and the Lens-Lievin road, but with the enemy holding Hill 65 they naturally dominated the battle, and constantly shelled our supply routes and mortared our trenches. **Another of the Fifty died here.** After this tour of duty the 5th Battalion's numbers were barely half strength, and they retired to the pretty village of Bouvigny on the slopes of Lorette Ridge. Here they stayed at Marqueffles Farm, not just to rest but also to train for an attack on Fosse 3, a large slagheap close to their earlier trenches at Lievin.

Marqueffles Farm on the slopes of the Lorette Ridge. The 5th prepared here for the attack on Fosse 3.

The attack on Fosse 3 started with a heavy barrage at 8.30pm on the 8th June 1917. One of our early shells hit an ammunition dump on the far side of the slagheap and a huge fire lit up the battle-scene.

Directly behind the buildings are the remains of Fosse 3, Lievin, where silhouetted against a red glow black figures waged war.

Silhouetted against the red-glow, black figures waged war with bayonet thrusts and hand-to-hand fighting, whilst others tossed grenades into enemy dugouts. Corporal Ted Lester, 'C' Company, was conspicuously gallant and won the military medal for his actions (see photograph). The War Diary confirmed that at least eighty Germans were quickly killed - mostly by bayonet. 2nd Lieutenant 'Bertie' Banwell, who had just returned from being wounded at Gommecourt, showed great leadership during the battle.

Front centre, Corporal Ted Lester with his section of C Company shortly before the attack on Fosse 3, June 1917.

The Germans launched a fierce counter attack and the 5th made an orderly withdrawal. The battle proved the full worth of a 'creeping barrage', whereby our shellfire, instead of ceasing at the time our infantry went 'over the top', crept forward and so kept enemy machine-gunners deep in their bunkers. At dusk on June 21st a tragic error by Canadian gas-operators killed twenty-four of our soldiers, and sixty-two others had to be sent to England because of their critical condition. The gas containers should have hit some mine buildings on Fosse 3, but human error resulted in two hundred of the projectiles landing in the trenches where 'C' Company were positioned for attack. They were almost wiped out - only their commanding officer, Captain Aubrey Moore M.C. survived - and that was because he was at home on sick leave. When he heard of the disaster he was inconsolable: *'My magnificent company has been wiped out.'* The gas used at this stage in the war was phosgene, and even if one survived, the scarring to eyes and lungs was irreparable. Many soldiers returned home and died a decade or more later as a direct result of this lethal gas. *'C'est la guerre.'*

Bullets brought back from France as souvenirs by Charles Hatter.

The 46th Division was now numerically very weak and in need of a rest, however, they were given the objective of capturing Hill 65, which overlooked Fosse 3. Three battalions were involved in the attack, these being the 4th and 5th Leicestershire and the 5th South Staffordshire. It was on June 28th at 7.20 pm that the creeping barrage started and the soldiers went over the parapet once again. The attack was a great success and despite some heavy shelling and counter attacking, they consolidated their position and Hill 65 was in their hands. On July 3rd they were relieved by the 25th Canadians and marched to Monchy Breton for a deserved rest.

The third week of July saw the 5th Battalion at Hulluch, now a relatively quiet sector about nine to ten

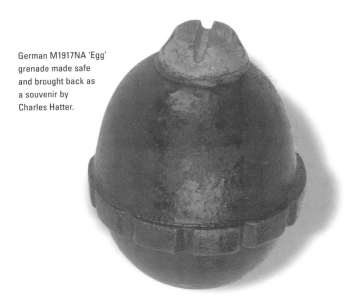

German M1917NA 'Egg' grenade made safe and brought back as a souvenir by Charles Hatter.

kilometres (six miles)) northeast of Loos. By this time the Division was approaching full strength thanks to new arrivals from England. A raid was planned to detract attention from a Canadian attack on Hill 70, a little to their south. On the night of August 16th at 10.30 pm the barrage started and the attack began at 10.58 pm. It was a very dark night and to avoid losing touch the officers called to each other. Our lads did a lot of damage to the enemy trenches but they in turn lost a good many men, some to our shells falling short. A leading casualty was Captain Charles Shields of 'D' Company, who was seriously injured, losing a leg. His remaining leg continued to trouble him for the rest of his life. He was a model soldier, full of energy and leadership and invariably was cheerful and positive. The trench raid was not looked upon as a success. Twelve men were killed, including Alfred Burton from Ellistown, three were taken prisoner and fifty-one were wounded.

The old killing fields of Hohenzollern at peace.

Following this raid the 5th took over trenches known as St.Elie Left, only a short distance from where the Battle of Hohenzollern Redoubt took place. Indeed, the infamous slagheap known as Fosse 8 still commanded the area. The whole district had seen fearful fighting, and huge mines had been detonated and both sides tried to occupy the craters as vantage points. Underground tunnels connected 'friendly' craters. Living in these tunnels was something new to the frontline soldiers. The tunnels were damp and slippery, the air was foul, in places it was impossible to stand upright and fungus grew everywhere. Conversely, the tunnels saved many lives, snipers could not operate and during a three-month stay the 5th lost only three wounded officers and eighteen men.

Early December 1917 and a short move to Cambrin Right, perhaps one-and-half kilometres to the northwest of St Elie. A quiet sector, and the 5th enjoyed a peaceful and restful Christmas in the village of Beuvry, near to Bethune. Some pigs were purchased and large quantities of pork, plum puddings (sent from Leicestershire for her troops), beer and wine were consumed. Beryl and I spent a sublime summer's day in Beuvry, and as we strolled along the pathways and entered the small shops, we often thought of those young soldiers having two days of Christmas joy amid a protracted and painful war.

A few rounds of German machine gunfire welcomed-in 1918, otherwise all was quiet. On January 6th a combination of incident and wretched luck resulted in the death of five men. All five were battalion runners - one had the D.C.M. and another the M.M. Three British aeroplanes collided in mid-air, and as they did so the enemy opened up with a few salvoes, and one shell landed on their headquarters, only two runners escaping.

Soon came heavy snowfalls and bitter night frosts. The braziers were kept topped-up with coke for hot drinks (and rum), so vitally important, especially during the early hours of the night when hypothermia could set-in.

In late January, the 4th (1/4th) and the 5th (1/5th) Leicestershire were topped-up with men from the 2/5th Leicestershire Battalion, because of a struggle to keep the first battalions up to operational strength. It also meant that some of the original (1914) members made a welcome return. (When soldiers were wounded and admitted for hospitalisation in England they were not always posted to their original units).

March of 1918 saw a Divisional increase in training of troops in the art of counter-attacking. Most notably, a civil-revolution resulted in our ally, Russia, withdrawing as a military power from the war, and senior military figures were alarmed at German troop movements from the Eastern to the Western Front.

The 5th Battalion returned to Cambrin Right Sector and noted the enemy was shelling with greater intensity, and their introduction of virulent 'mustard gas' to their weaponry. In the cold and snow the gas lay dormant but its essence was irremovable, and warm weather manifested its full and evil power. Just a little resulted in temporary blindness, loss of voice and painful blisters, a little more damaged internal organs resulting in a lingering death.

As was anticipated the German Spring offensive, 'Operation Michael,' began on March 21st and one week later the 46th North Midland Division marched to the Loos Sector to relieve the 46th Canadian Division. The enemy's artillery was highly active especially with gas shells, and Captain Aubrey Moore and forty-three other ranks suffered the effects and were hospitalised. The enemy swiftly broke through to the north, the old town of Bethune was shelled and seen to be in flames. Along the Loos Road is a village aptly named Philosophie, and the War Diary describes this coal-mining location: *There are few more desolate spots than Philosophie, on a dark wet night and when the horses have got the wind up.'* Back in 1918 it displayed scarred slagheaps, slime-filled shell craters, shattered cottages, the pungency of repeated gas attacks and

military graveyards. The rebuilt and redeveloped village still occupies both sides of the main Loos Road.

In the third week of April a debilitating and contagious illness spread to the Battalion ranks. It was a portent for 1919, when worldwide twenty million people died from that developing influenza strain. In a few days two hundred and fifty officers and men were admitted to hospital with symptoms that are now familiar. The War Diary declared that the illness was a mystery. The Medical Officer would not express an opinion.

The La Bassee Canal at Gorre.

From early May to mid-August 1918, the Battalion served at Gorre and Essars, two hamlets sitting either side of the La Bassee Canal. They were 4.5 kilometres (3 miles) northwest of Bethune. It was a relatively quiet spot, with occasional bouts of heavy shelling and plentiful supplies of gas. The canal was a summer bonus and racing galas were arranged near to the shade of a large old building, a brewery. **One of the Fifty** died here during heavy shelling.

The 5th Battalion crossed the canal and were in support for three days at Le Quesnoy, and on a light pastoral note, all available men were sent to cut corn to save it from spoiling. Bayonets not scythes were used and they reaped a bountiful golden harvest.

The Offensive, after early successes failed in its ultimate objective of reaching the Channel ports. After three years of war the Germans had suffered heavy losses, this led to a shortening of their line. To prepare for this 'retirement' they built reinforced-concrete defensive systems with natural height advantages, deep dugouts, powerful guns, excellent communication trenches and service lines. It was called the Hindenburg Line, and German Chiefs considered it to be impregnable. By the autumn of 1918 the 46th North Midland Division had earned an excellent reputation. The Division shared in failures, but by this date they were widely regarded as among the best, and certainly the most experienced Division on the Western Front. The St. Quentin Canal additionally strengthened the German Line, and the 'impossible' task of attempting to puncture and penetrate this Teutonic Barrier was allocated to the soldiers of the 46th.

At midnight on September 11th/12th the 5th Battalion entrained from Chocques Station, and left La Bassee to Lens Sectors for the last time, leaving many pals behind in corners of French fields. Their destination was over one hundred kilometres (75 miles) by train in a southeasterly direction, and a similar tangent from the battlefields of the Somme. On the 20th September 1918 the 5th Battalion, with assistance from two officers and forty men of the 4th, had the task of capturing Pontruet. This was a heavily defended village just to the north of St. Quentin. The stronghold was several kilometres ahead of the Hindenburg Line, and its guard was resolute and a thorn in the side to the Allied advance. At 5.00 am on September 24th a barrage signalled the intent as the men of Leicestershire (with the remnants of the Fifty) attacked the village. It was twilight and a thick mist made visibility poor, but that did not stop German machine-gunners from raking our 'jump-off' positions.

The 5th Leicestershire Batallion attacked from this field and immediately crossed the road near the memorial behind us.

The troops stormed across the Bellenglise Road and poured into the west of Pontruet, suffering casualties but making ground. The mist and battle-smoke caused some confusion with many heroic deeds being witnessed but never rewarded. An outstanding display of bravery, almost of self-sacrifice by Lieutenant J. C. Barrett won him the Victoria Cross. The citation reads,

'Owing to the conditions many men lost direction, and Lieutenant Barrett found himself advancing towards 'Forgan's Trench', which contained many machine-guns. Without hesitation he led a charge of men and was wounded on the way. In spite of this, he gained the trench and vigorously attacked the garrison, personally disposing of two machine-gun posts and inflicting many casualties. He was again wounded but climbed out of the trench in order to fix his position and locate the enemy. This he succeeded in doing and, despite exhaustion from wounds, gave detailed orders to his men to cut their way back to the battalion, which they did. He himself refused help, and was again wounded, so seriously that he could not move and had to be carried out. In spite of his wounds he managed to fight on, and his spirit was magnificent throughout. It was due to his coolness and grasp of the situation that any of his party were able to get out alive.'

(London Gazette, December 14th 1918).

The memorial at Pontruet where the 5th Leicestershire attacked from the field opposite as shown in the next photograph.

The Germans bombarded the British positions within Pontruet and furious hand-to-hand fighting occurred. At 7.30 pm, as the light was failing another charge was made. Our attacking front was so wide that some Sherwood Foresters entered the fray. The soldiers of the Battalion were drained after sixteen hours of battle, and annoyingly the relief battalion refused to enter the fray because of locational uncertainties. At 2.00 am on September 25th the 5th spent two hours in a tactical evacuation of the village. **Three of the First Fifty** did not survive.

Shortly afterwards General Boyd congratulated the 5th on their efforts. Although not totally successful, he stressed that they fully engaged superior numbers of German troops and prevented them from supporting a position to their right.

Beryl and I have visited Pontruet and in my opinion our soldiers fought brilliantly. They attacked an enemy three times their size that was 'dug-in' and held higher ground. The 5th lost a Company Commander, three subalterns, and thirty-eight other ranks killed. A further Company Commander and six subalterns were wounded, together with one hundred other ranks. One aspect of the battle was the initiative of each individual soldier, pressing on regardless of whether an officer or N.C.O. was killed or wounded, and demonstrating great ability with the bayonet. After retiring the enemy artillery dropped roughly one thousand shells of mixed calibre onto the Leicestershire positions.

On Sunday the 29th September 1918 at 5.50 am the heaviest barrage of the war smashed onto the Hindenburg Line. Many an officer believed that 'Dante's Inferno' was a comic strip by comparison. The awaiting troops downed their measures of rum and fixed bayonets. Around this time they chanted a little ditty, a soldiers' hymn before a charge.

'The bells of hell go ting-a-ling-ling

For you and not for me.

Oh, death where is thy sting-a-ling-a-ling

Or grave thy victory?'

The 137th Staffordshire Brigade led the charge against the German line in what was called the Battle of Bellenglise, and they were magnificent in spearheading the finest British victory of the Great War. The annals of history will forever remember the Staffordshire 'Terriers' and all of the soldiers of the 46th North Midland Territorial Division. After crossing the canal with lifebelts, lifelines and rafts the Allies poured over Ricqueval Bridge and pontoon bridges. The 5th Leicestershire and 5th Lincolnshire carried onto the next objectives whilst the enemy tried to re-organise and bring up reinforcements. The Leicestershire men captured eight large guns and took one hundred prisoners, having advanced about four miles. The men were pleased when they read that the 'Daily Mail' and other newspapers had given front-page headlines to their magnificent achievement.

A gradual advance through October 1918 continued against a stubborn enemy that fought for every village, and which regularly delivered high explosive as well as gas-shells, claiming lives on a daily basis, **including several of the First Fifty.**

The month saw beautiful weather, Captain Milne of the 4th Leicestershire Battalion wrote: *'An exhilarating nip in the morning air, bright sunshine at midday, a pleasant shimmering mist as the sun went to bed.'* As the two sister Leicestershire Battalions marched through the liberated French villages the civilians went wild with excitement and joy, throwing masses of flowers and petals all over their liberators.

On the eleventh hour of the eleventh day of the eleventh month the guns stopped firing. For a spell there was total silence, an unnatural silence until the soldiers heard the sweet whistling of the birds in the nearby orchards. After a few minutes of euphoria, other emotions surfaced, as individuals came to grips with losing relatives and friends during the four bloody years of battle. The Great War, which was to end all wars later proved not to be the case as their sons found out on September 3rd 1939. The two Battalions lost one thousand men from Leicestershire, with a further three thousand suffering from wounds and gassings that affected the remainder of their lives.

Twenty-two of the First Fifty survived but with most of them suffering for the rest of their days.

THE TIGERS

1915, well-worn boots, blistered feet and puttees tight.
Tiger badges enriched to old gold in the crimson evenin' sunlight.
Sturdy young men in khaki did toil under heavy load.
Mile upon mile down an endless Flanders road.
Esprit de corpse summoned power to mind and muscle.
Familiar songs and a wag played an old tin whistle.
They filed into trenches and followed signs to Leicester Square.
Bully beef and biscuits, time to reflect and maybe say a little prayer.

Concealment or shroud as a voluntary morning mist stood guard.
Mighty guns of volcanic power swallowed shells to regurgitate and bombard.
'Come on the Tigers,' came the officer's inspirational roar.
A thousand brotherly silhouettes from earthly trenches did soar.
Barbed wire the bloodied nails of the Devil's fingers!
Screeching shells a ghoulish harmony for insane singers!
Bravely onwards, step by step, and many fell in the battle-storm.
Smoke, gas, bullets and explosive elements of metallic form.

Spear-like lightning and thunderous clouds descended their way.
Bayonets and mortal wounds cleansed by rain as khaki fought grey.
Transfixed eyes bid farewell to soul-deep memories from within.
The Clock Tower, Granby Street, a county home and loving kin.
Death is the language when a body is broken.
Peace is the conveyance when words cannot be spoken.
1984, a Flanders farmer reaped a rich harvest by power of mind and muscle.
Familiar songs, as though a wag was playing an old tin whistle.

**Dedicated to the memory of all those who perished, and to all who fought
whilst serving with the (Royal) Leicestershire Regiment.**

Michael Kendrick.
May 2001

THE GHOSTS OF TRENCH 50

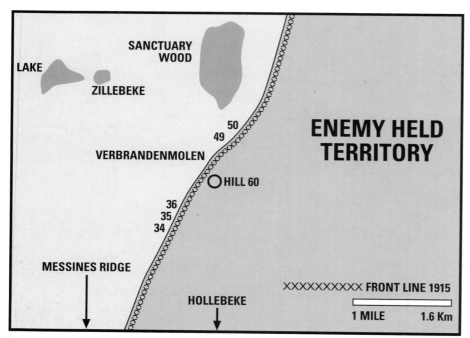

Having briefly visited Ypres beforehand, it was on the evening of the 29th June 1915 that the 5th Leicestershire Battalion occupied frontline trenches in the Salient. Captain J. D. Hills wrote, '*We reached the north side of Zillebeke Lake and followed a trench which gave us cover from Hill 60. At Zillebeke we left the trench and crossed a road at the double, on account of a machine-gun, which was permanently trained on it by the Boche. Then onwards past the church, another unpleasant locality, through a screened track to Maple Copse, an isolated little wood, and on to Sanctuary Wood, four hundred yards further on to the east. We then trekked to some old winter trenches numbered 46-50, which were only about two hundred yards from the enemy. Here we were shelled at least every three hours, and some part of the Battalion was receiving a whizz-bang at some time or another.*'

When one studies the map (for May 1915) of the location of Trench 50, it becomes clearer to see why several of the fifty and many other Leicestershire men lie buried in its vicinity, some beneath the trench itself. Occupying any frontline section in the Salient was highly dangerous due to enemy crossfire, especially with the Germans holding the higher ground, such as Hill 60. Losses were expected to be heavy. As the summer months of 1915 crept in, and the poppies bloomed, the enemy thrust forward and British sappers detonated a huge mine to counter them as fierce fighting took place around Hooge.

A pre-war territorial was the first man to be killed in Trench 50. Lance Corporal William (Bill) Barney of Ellistown was a respected young man, and nearly twenty-one years of age. Bill had joined the 5th Battalion on his eighteenth birthday in July 1912, and had proved his bravery in Lieutenant Moore's tunnelling team. Bill Barney was sniped on the night of June 30th and he lies in Sanctuary Wood Cemetery.

Looking on the south-west of Hill 60 are situated trenches 34, 35 and 36, in a territory known as Verbrandenmolen. These too became regular postings for the Leicestershire Terriers, with number 35 taking on the nickname 'Bomb Corner'. John George Bennett, one of the First Fifty, was killed in Bomb Corner by a whizz-bang on the 15th July 1915.

The men of the 4th and 5th Battalions were shaken by the massive mine exploded by allied tunnellers on the 19th July 1915. Private Charles Hatter recalled, '*The blast was terrific and for a long time debris fell from the skies around our trench, and some of it was clearly clothed in German grey.*'

The present day cratered and battle-scarred top of Hill 60.

A quiet moment in Trench 35 for an officer of the 5th Leicestershire Battalion during the summer of 1915.

A soldier of the 5th Leicestershire Battalion in Trench 35 in front of the devastation caused by shelling.

On July 23rd our tunnel team blew a mine under enemy trenches, opposite to our trench 50, and the reply came not too long afterwards. Captain J. D. Hills wrote: *'Stand-to passed off very quietly, when suddenly the ground heaved, dugouts collapsed and debris took to the skies. The end of our Trench 50 had been completely destroyed; it was just a deep crater, into which the Boche was firing trench mortars. Except for a few wounded men little could be seen of the garrison, they were buried and about eighty yards of our frontline no longer existed. Of 'B' Company alone the mine killed fifteen men and wounded twenty-seven others. Enemy mortars and rifle fire wounded another thirty men.'*

The barbed wire indicates the position of Trench 50, beyond the trees, would be the old German frontline. 250 yards to the right is a water-filled crater.

The narrow pale strip running west to east below the bungalow indicates the position of Trench 35, beyond which was the German frontline.

Private Owen Ward of the 5th Battalion, from Hathern near Loughborough, kept a personal war diary: *'One night we blew up a German trench, the first sap going up at 6.50pm. This was just short of the enemy frontline; the second sap went up at 7.00pm. What a sight. It was right under their frontline and the earth went up like a great mushroom. There then followed a bombardment lasting about 30 minutes and then things became quiet and we settled down for the night. At 8.00pm we posted our first night-sentries. After two hours, at 10.00pm, when our sentries were being relieved we felt the first shock. The earth seemed to lift in the air and a dull roar followed. I was knocked off my feet and flung about five yards into the communication trench at the back of us. The enemy had blown a mine under our trenches. All I could hear was moaning and groaning from men who were injured or buried. There were cries for help. I started to pull men out but it was dark and I was unable to see. Rifles were sticking out of the earth at different places - men were buried at the other end of them. A good number got out alive but alas many of our comrades were also dead. Reserves started to arrive to dig our frontline again. The enemy then tried to get into the crater that the exploded mine had created. Our bombers kept them at bay and when daylight came order was restored. The sight around us didn't look very promising, still, the digging carried on but some men were never found. (We made every effort to find them). A week later our Sappers were tunnelling to try and get into the crater when a surprise met them, another mine had been laid and was ready to be exploded. A corporal took charge and with a lot of risk to himself cut the wire, barricaded the sap and brought out all the explosives thereby saving quite a number of men's lives, including my own. The corporal won a D.C.M for his gallantry.'* (This was Corporal Jabez Emmerson, an Ellistown man).

In the corner of a foreign field, namely Sanctuary Wood. Here at rest with others are Harry Walker, Isaac Hall and Clifford Scott.

The cratered pool end of Trench 50 shrouded by trees. Dappled sunshine creates a peaceful and yet ghostly scene.

My wife and I have visited, on several occasions, the remains of the above trenches and we always remember the traumatic experiences of their past. Harry Walker was sniped during the dawn-chorus whilst on sentry duty on the 2nd July 1915. George Andrews, Walter Gray and Isaac Hall all died during the late-evening mine-blast of the 23rd, and Bill Massey was shot through the head during the early hours of August 8th. The teenage Clifford Scott was buried in a dugout by a shell on September 1st. The last six mentioned were in the First Fifty, and all died in trench 50, with John George Bennett in trench 35. Seven deaths during an eight weeks spell of horrific warfare.

A good deal of this area is now becoming increasingly wooded and the cratered end section of Trench 50 is now a deep pond, which we think of as a 'pool of peace'. Young trees shroud the pool, and dappled sunshine filters and flickers through the canopy to create a peaceful and yet ghostly scene. If perchance I saw an apparition of a young man in khaki, I wouldn't be in the least afraid; such lads sacrificed their lives for our freedom, and now lie under the still waters of peace. Other Leicestershire soldiers are at rest in a corner of a foreign field, known as Sanctuary Wood Cemetery, and all my wife and I could hear as we departed was the blackbird's evening song as the summer sun set on yet another July day.

THE BATTLE OF THE
HOHENZOLLERN REDOUBT

The soldiers of the 4th and 5th Leicestershire Battalions survived purgatorial conditions for four months within the Ypres Salient. Upon leaving this Sector they were warned that their next posting could be worse. The specific target was known as the Hohenzollern Redoubt, an enemy stronghold comprising of a huge low slagheap (Fosse 8) that was infested with machine-gun posts. Surrounding were buildings and cottages that were militarised and also a maze of sophisticated trench systems. Some of the defensive set-ups received names which later turned one's blood cold: 'Big Willie', 'Mad Point', 'Little Willie', 'Madagascar Cottages' and 'Fosse Trench'. The Redoubt was not unfamiliar to warfare; on the 25th September 1915 it was on the left flank of the powerful Allied thrust in the failed Battle of Loos, where so many Leicestershire men lost their lives.

The 13th October 1915 during the British artillery bombardment at Hohenzollern Redoubt. Fosse 8 can be seen in the background in the left half of the photograph. The white lines are the chalky trenches.

The above Battalions left the Salient and detrained at a station close to Bethune, in French Flanders, and made a base-camp at the village of Hesdigneul in early October 1915.

On October 12th our men marched the fifteen kilometres (ten miles) to the Redoubt in 'fighting order', with great-coats rolled and strapped to their backs. They arrived at 10.00 pm at Vermelles, and the following eight hours were spent packed solid in communication trenches. Each soldier carried six sandbags and every third a shovel. As you could imagine, none of them slept and the lucky ones had a drink before our artillery opened-up at noon on the

13th October 1915. The enemy artillery responded fifteen minutes later, and at 1.00 pm we released chlorine gas, and disastrously for us an enemy shell shattered some containers in our frontline. At 2.00 pm our troops, many wearing gas-helmets went 'over the top' and bayonet charged the enemy positions. Terrific machine-gun fire tore into them and a shrapnel barrage added to the heavy casualties. The heroism of Captain Langdale of the 5th appeared in the 'Daily Express':
'His men were ranged in the trench to his right and to his left waiting to go over the parapet. The Captain inspired his men by appearing totally relaxed, smoking his pipe whilst sitting on a campstool. He then lit-up again, took a few puffs, and rising to the parapet shouted: 'Come on Leicestershire' and the troops followed him.' Within twenty yards the attackers hit a wall of bullets, but it did not stop them all. The Captain showed immense bravery and leadership, continuing to urge his men on, until a bullet to the head mortally wounded him. The newspaper commented that, among the many deeds of this war, none stood out more than the charge of the Leicestershire men. Captain Hastings (an Ashby man) and 2nd Lieutenant H. J. Moss (from Nanpanton) led their men almost to the second enemy line until they were picked-off by sharpshooters. Captain Faire of the 4th was equally brave, until a razor-sharp piece of shrapnel entered his head and left through his shoulder. He died instantly. Hours passed and furious hand-to-hand fighting took place and repeated bayonet charges drove the enemy back, who in turn counter-attacked. Colonel Martin (of Woodhouse) showed remarkable bravery in leading his men of the 4th Battalion, even though he had been shot through the knee. He refused to leave the battlefield, and sat at the top of 'Bart's Alley' receiving reports and directing operations the best he could in the conditions. After darkness Lance Corporal Clayson of the 5th saved tens of lives by dragging wounded back to our trenches, and Captain Barton spent hours in No-Man's-Land giving morphine and water to the dying. When food and drink was brought-up during the night the men had

their first meal for twenty-four hours, but still no sleep. The morning of the Fourteenth was very misty and this became smog as the Germans continued to use shrapnel and gas shells throughout the day. It was at 8.00 am on the Fifteenth that relief was completed and buses took most of our troops back to Hesdigneul. There was a shortage of buses and seventy men of the 5th, led by Quorn's Major Toller had to march the ten miles back to base, arriving at midnight for a 'well earned rest.' The attack was a partial success in that the Redoubt was taken, but not Fosse 8, yet none of the attacking troops could be faulted.

There were the usual reasons given for the lack of success, failure of the artillery to destroy strong points such as 'Mad Point', the release of gas in a restless breeze resulting in greater suffering to the attackers, and the power of the enemy machine-guns. The total losses were: The 4th lost twenty officers and 453 other ranks as they were in the first attacking wave. The 5th lost 4 officers, 6 wounded, two gassed and thirty-five men killed, 132 wounded and 22 gassed.

Private Cato of Park Road, Coalville and Private Cross of Hugglescote wrote home telling of the dreadful battle and how their twenty-year-old pal,

Frank Woolhouse of the 5th had been killed. **Another one of the First Fifty** was killed on this day.

Other local men who died were:

Harry Allum of Ashby de la Zouch
Frederick Bartlam of Osbaston
Charles Betts of Sileby
James Biddles of Loughborough
Albert Brodribb of Moira
George Colver of Appleby Magna
George Fletcher of Ellistown
Lewis Gadd of Mountsorrel
George Gadsby of Ellistown
John Hall of Mountsorrel
George Henney of Ashby de la Zouch
Francis Johnson of Sileby
Ernest Newton of Shepshed
Ernest Pringle of Ashby de la Zouch
Thomas Squires of Loughborough
Francis Tunicliff of Castle Donnington
William Turner of Snarestone
George Waterfield of Loughborough
Albert Watterson of Mountsorrel
James Wileman of Measham.

———————————

Private Owen Ward, of Elm Cottage, Wide Street in Hathern, near Loughborough took part in the battle and shortly afterwards wrote the following poem which was found in his diary in 2003.

THE CHARGE ON THE HOHENZOLLERN REDOUBT

'Twas the 13th of October, when the Stirring Charge was made,
On the Hohenzollern Redoubt, by the Terrier's Brigade.
They'd held the line in Belgium for eight long, weary months,
They'd no chance to go forward, but they'd never drawn back once.
And now the chance was given them, each heart was filled with joy,
From the General Commanding to the youngest drummer boy!
We relieved the Guards at midnight; they explained to us the ground,
And how the trenches to the front with machine-guns did abound.
A Captain passed along the trench, 'Keep calm my lads,' said he,
'And by the help of God above we will claim a victory.'
The boys they understood him and already for the fray,
They cracked their jokes with n'er a thought of what might be 'fore-end of day!

At mid-day came an awful noise, like a hundred peals of thunder,
Our artillery had opened fire, 'twas like earth being sent asunder.
At one o'clock we gassed them, a harder death unknown,
But they, who make the horrors of war, shall reap what they have sown!
At five to two the order came, 'Stand to boys and get ready,'
'Tis hard this waiting for your doom, to be both calm and steady.
Again the order came along, 'Two minutes to go, now one,'
Then, 'over the top and at 'em lads, for God's sake do get on!'
In a very few minutes we found ourselves masters of their frontline,
Then it's: 'Over the top and at 'em again, go on you're doing fine.'
On 'No-Man's-Land' many a hero fell, and on, still on they came,
But their folks at home will feel proud to know, 'twas for Right and an honoured Name.'
The 'Gallant Lads' they held their ground, for two long days we're told,
And the Guards relieving were moved to tears at so many stiff and cold!

'Trust in God,' the chaplain said, 'And think of the badge you wear,'
They did, and they thought of their parents too, whose name they proudly bear!
The boys who were left held silent tears as they fight it o'er again,
For many a pal, ay, and brothers too are numbered with the slain,
But now we have gained the ground we want, but oh, what a lot we lost,
Still we did our duty, for the order was: 'Take and hold what'er the cost!'
If only the 'Slackers' in England would now think of those who are gone,
And resolve to shed their own life's blood for the sake of a dear old home.
If they would in one voice cry, 'I will,' then this terrible war would cease,
And the world at last would be clothed in a robe of everlasting peace.
Think of time in years to come when you've children of your own,
They ask: 'Did you fight in the War, Dad, so that I'd have an English home?'
You will proudly answer, 'Yes my lad, long before you came,
So that you might have an English home and bear an honoured Name.'

The Memorial Cross for men of
the 46th North Midland Division
who perished during the battle
of Hohenzollern Redoubt.

SOME OF THE SOMME

I have trodden the ground where the 46th North Midland Division attacked Gommecourt Wood on the 1st July 1916. Little has changed to this gentle undulating farmland since Mother Nature repaired the wounds inflicted by 'clay that walked tall'. I knelt on one knee and allowed the rich soil to pass through my fingers, for it is rich, rich in iron from the thousands of shells that exploded around this area. I feel it must also be rich in human worth, for so very many bodies were never found, simply returning to dust, but I believe it is a richer dust by far. I stood where the Sucrerie was located and thought of Captain Ward Jackson and the brave Company Sergeant Major J. R. Hill (of Coalville), and the fifty odd men who dug frantically to construct a trench there. I stood on the Gommecourt/Foncqueviller's Road and looked across the depth of the battlefield towards Pigeon Wood, wondering what passed through the minds of those young soldiers. They had been instructed to walk across No-Man's-Land, assured it would be little more than a stroll in the sunshine, *"The Barrage would have killed the Hun."* All too quickly they saw their friends, in some instances brothers, scythed-down by a multitude of machine-gun bullets. Some died instantly, others screamed in agony, but no one heard their death cries in the thunderous cacophony of the day.

The Great War Poet, Siegfried Sassoon wrote the following verse in: 'How To Die':

'Dark clouds are smouldering into red
While down the craters morning burns.
The dying soldier shifts his head
To watch the glory that returns;
He lifts his fingers toward the skies
Where holy brightness breaks in flame;
Radiance reflected in his eyes,
And on his lips a whispered name.'

How many sons, fathers and uncles died? How many wives suffered bleak and poverty-stricken futures without partners? How many children never saw their fathers again, and how many were never born, and literally for generations to eternity? The whisper from a dying breath, for the teenage soldiers it was probably 'mother', for others possibly a sweetheart or wife. My only consolation is that God willing there have been glorious reunions.

The attack was not a success, and even with hindsight it is difficult to see any other outcome, knowing the circumstances. Certainly as a decoy the attack was partially successful, with a few victories in the lower reaches of the Somme where the German defences proved less strong.

I wandered around Gommecourt Wood (illegally) and saw remains of the old German trenches and looked towards Foncquevillers. I can appreciate how the enemy gunners had a 'field day', because our advancing lads had no cover whatsoever. I strolled around the village; the locals smiled understandingly, having seen many pilgrims such as I before returning to Foncquevillers. I soon assessed where Midland Trench had been, and where the 5th Battalion came along Leicester Street communication trench just alongside the church. (See photograph in colour section). Close by I gazed in the direction of Gommecourt Wood, knowing this was the view our soldiers witnessed when the treacherous breeze blew-away their smoke screen. I started to walk in their footsteps and soon felt completely exposed, so conspicuous and worried in case an enraged farmer yelled at me to get-off his land. I thought of the 1st July 1916 and kept on, and fortunately was not disturbed. As I walked back the thousand yards or so the sun was beginning to set peacefully, whilst to the east it was dark and a flash of lightning streaked to earth and was followed by a rumble of thunder. Such is life, and I am pleased to have experienced such emotions and to feel compassion and understanding for my grandfather's generation.

EYES BY WHICH TO SEE

(May 1916 - A hospital in southern England)

Corporal Victor Wood (Military Medal) gazed through the hospital window.
His upper body elevated by a cross of pillows, his legs perpendicularly below.
At times breathing was rapid, shallow - lungs seared at Loos, gassed by chlorine,
Yet his eyes were focussed, be it on starlight or a picturesque springtime scene.

Private Edward Blythe lay horizontally; any other position brought violent pain.
He'd been a 'tunneller' and dug-deep below enemy lines in a fertile Flanders plain.
He'd eyes by which to see - but a head constrained by a heavy metal clamp,
And a field of vision revealed a cobwebbed ceiling and a patch of damp.

For several months Victor described the changing moods of day and night.
He took Edward's mind to scarlet sunsets and twinkling stars that shone bright.
Fresh green leaves that rippled in solar-beams and rustled in a gentle breeze.
A horse and dray, an omnibus, and the blacksmith's forge rendered by degrees.

'Edward, today the sky's pale-azure, and the sun's orchestrating a spectrum of colour.
The birds, I see blue, some gold crested, black and brown, and there's a warbler.
Five children are playing cricket on the dewy green and a mother is rocking her pram,
Whilst two old-timers cross Main Street to enter the 'Bulls Head' for a dram.'

'Victor, the orange glow of dawn, cherry blossom and golden fields of grain.
I yearn for the day when I may walk, once again, down an old English lane.
I don't think I'd have survived without your portrayal of real-life pleasures,
For only when it's impossible to partake, does one realise we live by half measures.'

Next morning Victor's bed was empty, he'd drifted in the night towards the stars!
As the weeks rolled-on Edward was able to sit up, assisted by two metallic bars.
He asked to be moved to the window, he longed to share the beauty of the view,
The view Victor described so vividly, he would now enjoy it too!

Two nurses pushed his bed towards the window and slowly he opened his eyes.
He saw, he saw - nothing, apart from a grimy factory wall; he uttered repeated sighs?
'Where, where are the scenes that Victor described, the green, the Bulls Head?'
'Edward,' said the nurse, 'he was blind and knew he'd soon be dead!'

Michael Kendrick
Any name association is strictly coincidental.

THE FIFTY - IN ALPHABETICAL ORDER

George. I. Andrews

George was born in December 1894 at Ravenstone. He was the second son of Mr & Mrs John Andrews, a painter and decorator and the family resided within the village, which is two kilometres west of the relatively new town of Coalville, Leicestershire. Upon leaving school he was employed as a miner at nearby Ibstock Colliery. George was a member of the Ravenstone Church Sunday School and later the Bible Class, and his pleasant and sincere attitude made him very popular.

His brother, John C. Andrews, born in 1890, was of a more serious nature and a regular soldier with the 1st Bedfordshire Battalion. He was a master-sniper, having won the prestigious gold cup at Aldershot in 1912. In early September 1914, Lance Corporal J. Andrews was sent to France in the British Expeditionary Force (B.E.F.), of one hundred thousand soldiers. They imperiously challenged the multitudes of German soldiers at Mons, with the Kaiser questioning their sanity - but not their bravery, by describing them as *'a contemptible little army.'* Great Britain's regular Army, although small in numbers was generally accepted as the finest in the world, and they put-up a stout resistance. Irony played a wicked part when John met his death. He was shot through the head by a German sniper on the 7th November 1914, dying instantly. (There were eighty thousand casualties in the B.E.F.)

George enlisted at Coalville in mid-August 1914 into the 5th (1/5th) Leicestershire Battalion.

With the other 49 recruits he spent nearly two months under canvas on the High Tor of Charnwood Forest, also training at the Drill Hall in Loughborough and the Institute at nearby Thringstone. On his final leave in early 1915 before embarking for France, George's last words to his distraught parents before he boarded the train at Coalville Station were: *'I will do my best to avenge my brother's death.'*

Shortly after Whit-Sunday, the 23rd May 1915, George wrote a letter home explaining how the Bishop of Pretoria had taken his confirmation vows on the battlefield. He continued that he attended his first communion on Whit-Sunday, on how he felt reassured and requested an auntie to forward a prayer and hymn-book to him. George was to spend nearly five months on the Western Front, as a private soldier in 'B' Company until his death, being killed instantly on the 23rd July 1915, aged twenty years. The Germans detonated a mine under his frontline trench (number 50), which was perilously close to the infamous Hill 60 in the Ypres Salient of Belgium. Captain J. L. Griffiths, his company commander, sent a letter to his parents explaining how George (2555) died: *'It is with much regret that I have to write to tell you of the loss of your son*

Private George Andrews on Friday night last. The enemy exploded a mine immediately under the trench where your son was standing. Every search has been made for him but unfortunately we have been unable to find him, and this will always be the case. We shall erect a cross where your son was last seen. George was a very good and cheerful soldier and will be much missed by his officers and comrades. Kindly accept my sincere sympathy and also that of the whole of my Company in your sad bereavement.'

The Coalville Times of the 6th August 1915 reports on his death and how badly it disturbed the Ravenstone community. More details relating to his death can be found elsewhere in the book. George's name can be read on the War Memorial in Ravenstone Churchyard.

Major Baker

Major was the third son of Mr & Mrs Joseph Baker, and was born in 1896 at Hugglescote.

His father was employed as a deputy at the South Leicestershire Colliery in Ellistown, and on leaving school he became a collier at the same pit. The family lived on the Ashburton Road at Hugglescote and he worshiped at Ebenezer Baptist Chapel and Sunday school on the Ashby Road, Coalville. Several of the Fifty did likewise, and remained very close friends until death parted them. Major (2431) enlisted at Coalville in the first week of the war into the 5th Leicestershire Battalion; however, by April of 1915 he was serving with the 2/5th (Reserve) Battalion. He may have been wounded whilst with the 1/5th, or illness may have prevented him from embarking with them for France, and hence his reposting.

On the 23rd April 1915 the Pastor at Ebenezer Chapel read out his name from the Roll of Honour,

together with thirty-eight others who were serving in the Armed Forces.

Major would have been involved in subduing the Easter Irish up-rising in Dublin in 1916, and in March 1917 was near to Mericourt on the Western Front. It was reported in the Coalville Times of the 4th May 1917 that he was very badly wounded. Lance Corporal Major Baker wrote a letter to his parents, explaining that both of his feet had been amputated due to the seriousness of the injuries received. He also stated that he was hospitalised in France, but hoped to return to England shortly.

Major married Francis Tutt of Newcastle. He died in a military hospital at Ayr, Scotland in 1964. He was a first cousin to Walter Baker below.

Walter Saddington Baker

Walter was born on the 5th November 1889, and spent his early years at 12, Hotel Street, Coalville. Around 1892 the family took the short trip to 16, and then to 20, Park Road. He was educated at the Coalville British School, based at the London Road Baptist Chapel, and subsequently at the Wesleyan School on Belvoir Road. The latter school possessed the excellent Mr Thomas Frith as teacher, and Walter learned Pitman shorthand and typing skills by the tender age of 12. At the age of fourteen he was so proficient that he was teaching them to adults at a nearby night school. A very able and intelligent young man, he also taught piano and organ, which again he mastered at a relatively young age. Undoubtedly it helped that he was the son of an accomplished musician.

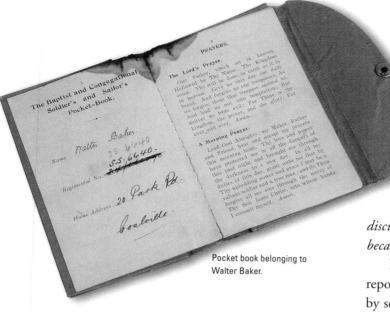

Pocket book belonging to Walter Baker.

When he left school he became a costing clerk at Stableford's Wagon Works, Coalville, and studied to become a draughtsman through a correspondence course. Walter enlisted at Coalville in mid-August 1914 into the 5th Leicestershire Battalion. Major Baker, above, was his first cousin and like Major, Walter had his name read out from the roll of honour at Ebenezer Chapel in April 1915.

Whilst at Luton an officer noted his sharp-mind, his secretarial and administrative skills, which were much sought-after in 1914, and senior officers decided he would be of greater benefit serving elsewhere. On the 1st April 1915, Walter was sent to Aldershot to familiarise himself with various military techniques and methods, before progressing for further staff training at the Army Service Corps in Kensington, London. He was then posted to the 52nd Lowland Division, half their numbers of which had already fought with the British Expeditionary Force in France since 1914. His primary role involved the planning and logistics for the remainder of the Division to embark for the Mediterranean.

Walter departed from Liverpool Docks on the 21st May 1915 aboard H.M.T. 'Mauritania', and no doubt gave due consideration of his future destination, the Dardanelles. The troops arrived at this far-eastern section of the Mediterranean, just off Mudros on the 29th May 1915, and dug in at Cape Helles on June 6th. The Coalville Times of the 2nd July 1915 proudly reported: *'Congratulations to W. S. Baker on his promotion. Sergeant Baker (SS 6640) is serving with the Mediterranean Fleet and has witnessed some exciting*

scenes during the bombardment of the Dardanelle's Forts. We hope to report soon some of his experiences.' He was later promoted to staff sergeant under the command of Sir Ian Hamilton, the leader of the expedition, and became involved with the successful evacuation plans for December 1915.

Walter's son, local historian and author, Denis Baker said: *'My father would never discuss the Dardenelle's Campaign against the Turks because it was such a horrific tour of duty.'*

Its reputation now goes before it. Eyewitnesses reported some of the old battleships being ripped apart by sea-mines, with many sailors drowning. During the 'landings' the sea was red with the blood of Allied troops, as their stomachs were ripped-open by barbed wire hidden beneath the waves at the jump-off points. Others were scythed-down by enemy machine-gun fire from nests situated on higher ground. During the long summer months the heat was intense, the smell of death appalling, food and especially water rations short, dysentery was rife and men were coated in flies and lice. Towards the end of the year came a deluge of rain, followed by heavy snow and many troops were crippled by frostbite (they still wore tropical uniforms).

It is well documented that the finest aspect of the Campaign was the brilliantly thought-out and executed evacuation (retirement) plan, which completely fooled the Turks. Walter almost certainly would have had an involvement with this plan and he deserved the credits he received. They left Mudros and arrived in Egypt at the beginning of February 1916. Billeted in Cairo for a week, they were involved in the defence of the Suez Canal at Port Said. On February 27th Walter's Brigade (155), entrained for Kantara to set up outposts twelve kilometres (seven miles) to its east, to defend caravan routes through the desert. There was an occasion when an overwhelming Turkish cavalry force attacked a desert garrison where Walter was stationed. All the defending occupants had to fight for their lives in the ensuing battle, and the Turks suffered heavy casualties. An enemy officer surrendered his pistol to Walter, and for many years he kept it as a memento of a life-or-death struggle. During the middle-east conflict Walter, and most of his companions, suffered terribly health-wise with several attacks of malaria and dysentery.

A wearying campaign developed, and by December 1917 the Brigade had battled doggedly right up to the gates of Jerusalem. Unfortunately, following this dramatic success they were then immediately dispatched to the Western Front. Denis Baker said: *'My father was a devout man, and he felt much regret never to have had the opportunity to enter the Holy City, and instead found himself posted to the Arras Sector of France in a European winter.'*

Later the Allies fought-off the German Spring Offensive of the 21st March 1918 onwards, and then began the final advance to victory.

 After 3 years the staff sergeant received his first leave of the war, and joyfully returned home to marry Fanny Kirkland Price on the 5th June 1918. The couple had two sons, Colin Price Baker, who sadly died in childhood and Denis Walter Baker. Fanny's father, William Price played a key role with the search party for the Whitwick mining disaster of the 19th April 1898. He was under-manager at Ibstock Colliery, and had worked in the pits from the age of nine, and was later an under-manager at Whitwick Colliery until his death on the 14th April 1935, at 77 years of age.

In July 1918 Walter returned to the Western Front and assisted in the final push for victory. Walter was very proud as 155 Brigade led the ceremonial entry parade into Mons, Belgium, on the 15th November 1918; it was the same town that the initial conflict had started in 1914.

After assisting in the wind-down of regimental affairs he was finally demobbed in February 1919. His outstanding contribution to the war-effort deservedly earned a Meritorious Service Medal and a 'Mention in Despatches.' When he left 155 Brigade his commanding officer, Brigadier General G. H. Harrison supplied him with a glowing testimonial.

After four-and-a-half years military service he returned to his office duties at Stableford's. The Coalville firm manufactured railway-train wagons for the Indian State Railways. Walter found it somewhat

ironic that one of the trains blown up by the celebrated 'Lawrence of Arabia' during the Desert Campaign had wagons bearing the Stableford nameplate. The ill fortune that is often around the corner surfaced just when Walter was scheduled to take charge of the costing office. Stableford's had been struggling with the order situation for some time; however, it was still a massive shock for the town when the firm went into receivership in 1927. The main reason for its closure was the Indian Railway's decision to make its own waggons. In addition there was a lack of capital investment in the U.K. By the time Walter and Fanny had moved to their new family house, 182, Forest Road, Hugglescote, (which he designed himself), he had obtained a new position at 'En-Tout-Cas Ltd', in Syston. Unbelievably, for four years he bicycled to-and-from work (a round trip of forty kilometres--twenty five miles) until obtaining the position of Assistant Relieving Officer for Ashby de la Zouch District. In October 1933 he was appointed Deputy Registrar of Births and Deaths, then Deputy Registrar of Marriages. By 1945, the end of World War 2 he was Deputy Registrar for Coalville. For very many years he was Organist and Deacon for Ebenezer Baptist Chapel at Coalville, and was closely associated with such friends as my mother's folk. During 1939-45 the heavy movement of wartime evacuees vastly enlarged his duties as Relieving Officer, and as a result health problems were beginning to resurface, mainly as a result of his health-sapping war-years. He was also having periodic fainting bouts, and specialists diagnosed the problem as myocarditis (heart disease). It was during the dreadfully long and cold winter of 1947, following an attack of pneumonia that further weakened him, that he quietly succumbed after a determined struggle, aged only fifty-eight years. A packed Ebenezer Chapel paid respects to a fine man.

Denis is a good friend (we are also distantly related), and I find it very moving that Walter was sitting to the right and alongside my grandfather, Charles Hatter, on the photograph of the Fifty. They were friends, and their descendants ninety years down the line, also.

William Baker

William was born in October 1897 at Stamford in Lincolnshire. His father, George, took his family to Leicestershire to enable him to obtain employment at Ellistown Colliery. They lived at 2, Ashburton Road, Hugglescote (next door to Wilfred Robinson of the Fifty) and William worshipped at St. John the Baptist Church and was educated at the Church School, which was (and is) just across the road. Frederick John Wainwright (1874-1966) was a teacher there for many years and finally the headmaster from 1911-34; he later was Church Warden from 1923-54.

William was a clever and sensible lad and upon leaving school he followed his father down the mines, obtaining a job at Bagworth Colliery. Young William enlisted at Coalville in mid-August 1914 into the 5th Leicestershire Battalion and although only sixteen years of age (nearly seventeen) he was accepted following a white lie. At that time William was living at Page's Hill in Hugglescote.

During service with the 5th Battalion, William (2554) was wounded and hospitalised for a time. When fully recovered he was reposted to the 1st Leicestershire Battalion (40739), and died of wounds near to Loos in France on the 5th September 1917.

William, the 'company orderly', was accompanying his Commanding Officer to the trenches when a shell-explosion killed him instantly.

There came added sadness for the family when his senior officer failed to send a letter expressing sorrow upon his death. Eventually his sister wrote to the authorities asking for confirmation of his death, and a junior officer wrote to apologise and explain the delay.

It transpired that the same shell badly injured their commanding officer (C.O.). He went on to write that the colonel had placed great confidence in William, hence the importance of the post he held, and that the Battalion appreciated to the full his fine qualities as a British soldier. The Coalville Times reported that he signed on at the first recruitment meeting at the Olympia Theatre in mid-August 1914. William had a sister and also a brother, George (Lance Corporal, 37846, 1st Reserve Oxford and Bucks Light Infantry who survived) who was serving in the Forces in India. William was only nineteen years of age when he met his violent death after serving two and a half years on the Western Front. His name can be read on the Coalville Clock Tower Memorial, and also on a tablet in St. John The Baptist Church at Hugglescote.

James Bancroft

James was born in the 1890s at Thringstone, near Coalville. He lived on John Street and regularly attended St. Andrew's Church. James enlisted at Coalville in mid-August 1914 into the 5th Leicestershire Battalion. He was wounded in 1915, treated in France and hospitalised in England, and upon recovery was reallocated to the 8th Leicestershire Battalion (110th Brigade of the New Army). The Battalion was in trenches at Epehy on the Cambrai Sector of France when the Germans launched their huge Spring Offensive on the 21st March 1918. (The War Diary noted that the enemy had shown increased activity since the turn of the month). At 2.30 am the 110th Brigade was shaken by a heavy enemy barrage of both high explosive and shrapnel shells. As dawn broke thousands of German storm-troops attacked through the mist and drove the Leicestershire soldiers back.

Throughout the day the battle raged in Epehy, hand-to-hand fighting from one street to the next, with ruined houses and cellars proving excellent cover for both sides, especially snipers.

As the cover of night descended the enemy launched another heavy barrage to prevent allied reinforcements from reaching the battlefront, and eventually the town fell into German hands. Those of our troops that managed to escape began a long and weary retreat - sleeping in ditches and constantly being harassed by shellfire. It is no longer possible (if ever) to learn what happened to Private James Bancroft (2564-240636) who lost his life on that day.

At the beginning of April 1918 the Brigade was fighting in the Ypres Sector.

James's name is remembered on the War Memorial Plaque in St. Andrew's Church.

Frederick Bartlam

Frederick, or perhaps 'Fred' was born in the 1890s in Osbaston, a village some ten kilometres (seven miles) south of Coalville, and two kilometres east of the historic small town of Market Bosworth. Frederick was residing in Coalville and had many friends and associates in the town. His mother was a resident of Osbaston, however his father had died on the 8th July 1914. Whether his death influenced Frederick's decision is uncertain, but he enlisted at Market Bosworth in mid-August 1914 into the 5th Leicestershire Battalion. Frederick (2561) was one of many Leicestershire soldiers who fell at the charge in the Battle of Hohenzollern Redoubt on the 13th October 1915. More details can be found elsewhere in this book.

The Coalville Times published notice of his death on the 10th December 1915, and informed readers that he was one of the original First Fifty and was very popular with all his associates.

A rare name, but in spite of telephone calls and letters to Bartlams within the neighbourhood, no connection could be made. The sad end of a line.

Frederick's name can be read on the Memorial in the Market Place of Market Bosworth.

Cecil Thomas Beadman

Mr & Mrs Thomas Beadman and their sons moved into the area from East Grinstead in Sussex, a large village about eight kilometres (five miles) east of Salisbury.

Cecil was their first-born son in 1895 and his brother, Roy, in 1898. In the early years of the twentieth century they moved to northwest Leicestershire, setting-up home on Forest Road, Hugglescote. Coalville Co-operative Society employed Thomas and the family worshipped at St. John The Baptist Church where the minister was Canon Henry Broughton. The sons were also educated at the Church School.

Cecil was regarded as a pleasant, clever and serious-minded lad, who was always very attentive to detail. He studied at evening classes and passed Board of Education Examinations in Drawing. Roy possessed all of his elder brother's qualities and attributes. Due to his exceptional ability and efforts, Cecil was employed as a draughtsman in the drawing office of Wootton Brothers, an internationally known iron-works company. Samuel Boot, father to his good friend, Sam (junior), worked on a lathe for the same company.

The Beadman family was settled, happy, and liked and respected within the community - until the candle of life started to flicker disconcertingly. Mrs Beadman died suddenly in July 1914, and whether or not this had any bearing, but in the middle of the following month Cecil enlisted at Coalville into the 5th Leicestershire Battalion. He was well liked in the Battalion and promotion was in the offing, when a chill-wind flickered the candle yet again on the night of the 14-15th May 1915. Cecil was in a large party of battalion-men digging a much-needed new trench at Zillebeke in the Ypres Salient. The War Diary states: *'All digging records were broken as a consequence of enemy fire.'* The Germans could hear the digging and randomly raked the inky-dark area with machine-gun fire. Cecil (2566) was killed by a burst of bullets and died instantly. Lieutenant Aubrey Moore sent a letter on May 21st to Thomas Beadman: *'I can assure you that your son died instantly. He was most popular both with officers and men and we feel his loss most bitterly. I can testify that he was a true soldier and man. I could always rely on him to do anything, no matter how difficult, and he feared nothing. He laid down his life for his country and he died like a soldier and a man. Again I offer my deepest sympathy and that of other officers.'*

The Coalville Times of the 28th May 1915 confirms the death of a 'Hugglescote Territorial' and the detail about him being one of the First Fifty. Cecil was just twenty years of age.

Roy won a scholarship from the Church School to Coalville Grammar School, and in 1914 obtained employment as a clerk at the Swadlincote branch of London City and Midland Bank, when he was called-up. As far as Thomas was concerned the candle was finally stubbed out in 1917. Roy was quickly promoted to a lance corporal in the Leicestershire Regiment, part of Kitchener's New Army, and was just nineteen years of age when he complained of feeling unwell. Following an examination by a medical officer he was sent to a hospital in southern England, dying shortly afterwards from cerebro-spinal meningitis in May 1917. Thomas, having lost a wife and two sons in less than three years decided to leave the district, and moved to Penge in south London in an attempt to rebuild his life.

Cecil is buried near to his best pal, Sam Boot, at Lindenhoek Chalet Military Cemetery, just to the south of Kemmel. The brothers' names can be read on the Coalville Clock Tower Memorial, and also on a tablet in St. John The Baptist Church, Hugglescote.

George Harry Bennett

George was born in the 1890s in Pike Street, Shepshed. His daughter, Florence Storer smiled as she said: *'All of his life he comically referred to it as 'Pig Street.'* The village, the largest in England is six kilometres (four miles) west of Loughborough.

Little is known of George's father and his mother Elizabeth Anne, (nee Hartington) was to die at an early age. It was left to his elder sister, Anna, to care for him and to bring him up. (Such was the hardship of those times).

Later Anna married the son of Thringstone's John Hall, Ernest Hall. He was a collier but also an ex-regular and reservist for the 2nd Leicestershire Battalion. They lived at 20, Talbot Street, Whitwick, a village now adjoining Coalville. Anna, continued to care for young George and treated him as a son, as did the warm-hearted Ernest. Their marriage was blessed with three daughters; Ernest called them his little birds.

George Bennett and sister Anna soon had to cope with a further family bereavement when their brother-in-law, Charlie Hall, died of Bright's Disease (a complaint of the kidneys) when he was just twenty-one years of age.

Florence informed me that her father, George, met his future wife, Elsie May Atkins, in Filbert Street at Leicester, but it's unclear whether they went to a football match or some other social activity. Elsie at the time was living at 138, Belper Street, Leicester and with love blossoming they married at Whitwick Methodist Chapel on Boxing Day 1912. They had four children, Charles being born in 1914, George in 1919, Florence in 1922 and Ursula in 1926. Florence smiled as she informed me that Ursula has always been referred to by the nickname, 'Chick'. The reason was because at the time her mother gave birth in an adjacent bedroom, the other children swore they heard a chicken-like noise. (A little bird nevertheless).

George Bennett seated left in 1916.

The 4th August 1914 changed the lives of the Bennett and Hall families forever. Ernest Hall received a telegram ordering him to report to his battalion immediately. George was a collier, and about a week later enlisted at Coalville into the 5th Leicestershire Battalion. In early 1915, Elsie sent a photograph of her and baby, Charles, from 138, Belper Street, Leicester, *'With fondest love from your ever loving wife, Elsie.'* Ernest frequently wrote to his Anna, thanking her for letters and parcels containing amongst other things, cake, which he shared with his comrades in arms.

In February 1915 Ernest wrote:

'Jack Storer is with me at the front, he used to work for Enoch Briers. I'm all right but I wish it would get a bit warmer. I always said I would be in something big, but I didn't think it would be like this; still it's all in a good cause. I am sorry to say some of my pals have gone under, but I don't think it will go on for much longer.

Tell my little birds that their dad will come home some day. I shall not be sorry when.'

Elsie Bennett and her son Charles, 1915.

during this stay a Reverend George Woolcock housed his wife Elsie, and Charles (a babe in arms). The reverend was so charmed by the pair that before they left he presented Charles with a small picture that he had painted. To this day it is still a treasured item within the family. The serious bullet injury to his left arm was a 'Blighty' and he received a war pension of five shillings per week (twenty-five new pence) for the rest of his life. (Blighty comes from the Hindi word, bilayati meaning: foreign country). He received an honoury discharge on the 18th June 1918. George returned to his family home at 190, Talbot Street, Whitwick, and as I mentioned earlier the couple had three more children. Life was indeed particularly hard for colliers in the nineteen twenties and thirties.

His left hand was 'locked like a claw', but he had a steely determination and proved he could still work down the mines. He was involved in the Miners' Strike of 1926 and was a good friend of Hugglescote man, Charles Hatter (A Union man and another of the Fifty).

Dreadful news arrived when Ernest Hall was killed whilst serving with the 2nd Leicestershire Battalion at the Battle of Neuve Chapelle, France. The battle raged for several days and on the 13th March 1915, a day of heavy shelling and sniper fire he was mortally wounded. Anna received a letter from a friend of her husband's on March 31st conveying the news that he was dead (earlier missing). An official letter dated 2nd April 1915 confirmed this. Ernest worked at Whitwick Colliery and he was the first Whitwick soldier to be killed in the war. He was not to be the last. The Coalville Times of the 5th April 1915 solemnly discloses the death of the Whitwick soldier. Anna, with children of six, four and a babe in arms remarried in later life.

Further dreadful news followed on the 23rd July 1915, when Ernest's younger brother, Isaac Hall, another of the First Fifty was killed with others when the trench he was in (trench 50) was blasted apart by an enemy mine.

George suffered the hell-like conditions of 'life' on the Western Front. He was a frontline soldier at battlefronts Ypres, Hohenzollern (Loos), and Vimy Ridge. He was wounded at Gommecourt on the opening day of the Battle of the Somme, 1st July 1916. (There were sixty thousand British casualties on that day alone, mostly in the first hour of battle). A bullet ripped through his forearm, permanently damaging guides, tendons, etc.

Following his initial treatment at Boulogne Hospital he was forwarded to York Hospital, and

George in civvies, 1924.

A truly interesting book could be written on the survival instincts, and colourful activities of George's nocturnal exploits - poaching rabbits and game birds. For this end his faithful dog 'Nance', a whippet, served him admirably. The old warrior was happy enough and continued to work hard until he was struck down by T.B. (Tuberculosis) in 1940. The following four long years of World War 2 and rationing did not help, and in-spite of his strong will and Markfield Sanatorium's greatest efforts, he succumbed in 1945 to what was largely an incurable illness at that time. Florence also caught the illness but regained complete health. George's wife, Elsie was to die in 1969 from heart disease.

Many thanks to Florence Storer, daughter of George and Elsie and also to his granddaughter, Pauline Pollard. Florence is so pleased that her father's name will be remembered along with the other forty-nine.

John George Bennett

Always called George, but not related to the above. He was born on the 3rd April 1895 at Hugglescote. The eldest son of Mr Joseph R.Bennett, a cashier at Whitwick Colliery, a Coalville overseer and a former member of the Urban Council. Later the Bennett family lived on Berrisford Street in Coalville and George went to the local Wesleyan School on Belvoir Road. He was also a chorister at the Coalville Primitive Methodist Church, and attended St. John The Baptist Church at Hugglescote. Upon leaving school he obtained a job as a fitter at Wootton Brothers, internationally known Iron Works Company. He enlisted in his hometown in mid-August 1914 into the 5th Leicestershire Battalion. George met his death on the 15th July 1915, aged just twenty years at Trench 35, infamously labelled as 'Bomb Corner' near to Hill 60 in the Ypres Salient of Belgium. The War Diary for that date: *'Whizz-bangs (trench mortars) were particularly disagreeable on this day.'*

Last Letter to Home

George's last letter home was dated the 11th July 1915:

I am writing to say that we are off to the trenches in all probability tonight. I don't feel very well, but if I land up there all right I shall be better. Thanks very much for the parcel, but I don't feel like eating much at present. The reason is I cannot keep anything down. Anyhow, one cannot always feel up-to the mark, but it makes it rather bad, as you have to get along just the same, unless you are absolutely done. The weather is dull here and generally fair. We are not far from the 1st Leicester's and I have seen several Coalville chaps - William Eames, Sam Allen, Tom Palmer, etc.

I can't tell you any more as it is posting time, so remember me to all the neighbours and give my love to the kiddies. Wish me the best of luck.

Your ever-loving son, George.'

Mr. J. Bennett received confirmation dated the 23rd July 1915 from the Record Office at Lichfield:

'It is my painful duty to inform you that a report has been received this day from the War Office notifying of the death of No 2558, Private J.G. Bennett, of the 1/5th Battalion of the Leicestershire Regiment. The death occurred on the field of battle and I am to express to you the sympathy and regret of the Army Council on your loss. The cause of death was wounds." Another letter arrived: *'The King commands me to assure you of the true sympathy of His Majesty and the Queen in their sorrow. 'Kitchener.'*

Letter from one of the Fifty

A good friend of George, Cecil Bradshaw, wrote home on the misunderstanding that George had survived his wound:

'Just as it was breaking day George got up to fire at a loop hole (he was one of our best shots), and was taking aim for another shot when he was hit.

I picked him up and did my best before they carried him away. The last I heard he was in hospital and then I was told incorrectly that he had died.

Tell Mr & Mrs Bennett that all in the platoon miss him very much. He is a good chap and not a bit nervy.'

George's pre-war employer, Mr. John Wootton sent a letter to his parents:

'I am very sorry to hear of the sad loss you have sustained in the death of your son.

While the lad was with us in our shops we found him a good boy and always attentive to his duties, and hoped in the near future to see him return. You have the satisfaction of knowing that he did his duty here, and as a man and a soldier, and I trust you will be able to let this console you. Kindest regards to you all.

Yours sincerely, John Wootton.'

The Coalville Times of the 30th July 1915 prints the details of the death of one of the Fifty.

George's name can be read on the Coalville Clock Tower Memorial, and on a tablet in St. John The Baptist Church at Hugglescote.

Harold Groves Blackham

Harold was born in 1893 at Smethwick, which is now a suburb about five kilometres due west of Birmingham city centre. He was the son of Mr. A. P. Blackham, Conservative Agent for southeast Derbyshire who lived at Stavely, a village six kilometres (four miles) northeast of Chesterfield in Derbyshire. Harold was living in digs in Hugglescote, and worshipped at St. John The Baptist Church. He enlisted at Coalville in mid-August into the 5th Leicestershire Battalion. He was employed as a clerk for Mr. W. Baldwin, the Conservative Agent for the Bosworth Division of Leicestershire. The War Diary states: *'The Battalion was in the Messines Sector of Belgium with the headquarters in nearby Kemmel. Colonel Jones had found a new home for himself in the village - a small shop in a lesser street. He had been there for less than twenty-four hours, when at mid-day on the 4th June 1915, the Germans started to bombard the area with their deadly 5.9 inch shells. The colonel was in discussion with Colonel Jessop of the 4th Battalion, just outside of the house, with two orderlies Robert Bacchus (1441) a pre-war Territorial from Rempstone, and Harold Blackham (2553) holding the two horses close by. The very first shell that came over exploded amongst them. Colonel Jones was injured in the hand, neck and thigh, whilst the other three men were killed, so too the horses.'*
He was just twenty-one years of age. When his father received notification of his death he wrote:
'Such sympathy as we have received helps us to bear our sorrow. It is gratifying to know that our dear lad was so beloved, and we have the satisfaction of knowing that he died nobly, fully prepared to meet his God, in the cause of freedom, King and country. He died for others.'

The Coalville Times of the 25th June 1915 identified the death of another of the First Fifty. Harold's name can be read on the Coalville Clock Tower Memorial, and on a tablet in St. John The Baptist Church at Hugglescote.

Edgar Ewart Boot

Edgar was born in 1894 at Coalville. He was the son of Mr & Mrs Arthur Boot of 43, Park Road in the town. Edgar attended Christ Church Bible Class (see his photograph in Thomas Catlow's section) and played for their successful league championship side of 1909-10, alongside Walter Handford and Thomas Catlow, two more of the Fifty. After leaving school he was employed at Stableford's Wagon Works until he enlisted at Coalville in mid-August into the 5th Leicestershire Battalion. Edgar was badly gassed during the charge at the Battle of Hohenzollern Redoubt on the 13th October 1915, and received three months treatment at Manchester Hospital. The Coalville Times of the 7th January 1916 commented that, Edgar, one of the Fifty, was much improved and would soon be returning to Battalion Headquarters. Shortly afterwards he was instructed to report to Grantham for training and was subsequently posted to the 30th Reserve Company, 5th Battery of the Machine-Gun Corps.

He received promotion to corporal with the service number 58972, before once again being wounded and forwarded for hospitalisation in England. Edgar survived the conflict and in 1919 returned to work at Stableford's, and at the time of its closure in 1928 held a senior position within the company. He had a brother, Maurice, who was a 2nd Lieutenant in the Royal Flying Corps, and happily he too survived the war.

Details of the Battle of Hohenzollern Redoubt can be found elsewhere in the book.

Edgar was a life-long friend of Charlie Hatter and he sits on Charlie's right in the photograph taken on the 30th October 1914.

Enquiries led to an assumption that at best there is only a distant relationship with Ernest Samuel Boot.

Ernest Samuel Boot

Always known as Sam. He was born at Hugglescote in 1897 and attended St. John The Baptist Church and the nearby Church School. His parents, Samuel and Francis Boot had four other children, John William, Harry, Zillah and Mary. Later in life the family moved to 104, Melbourne Street, Coalville. (Now demolished, the house stood on the corner of Bridge Road, opposite to where the Coalville Times office stands). Sam received his latter education at the local Wesleyan School on Belvoir Road. Samuel senior operated a lathe at Wootton Brothers Iron Works, and young Sam's best friend, Cecil Beadman was a draughtsman at the same company. (The building was demolished in 1981 to make way for the Co-Operative Super-Market). Samuel senior was also secretary to the Liberal club for many years, indeed his son, John William took over the same position at a future stage. Sam was working at Stableford's Wagon Works at the outbreak of the war

He volunteered at Ashby de la Zouch, perhaps thinking he'd be less known there, he was only a little over seventeen years of age. With the customary white lie he was accepted, and was far from being alone with such a falsification. Sam had a strong character and he was full of enthusiasm to fight for the kingdom of his birth. With youthful enthusiasm he was confident that a spell in the army would be full of excitement and adventure, and besides everyone said it would be over by Christmas 1914.

After receiving his uniform in October at Loughborough's Drill Hall, he returned home and had his photograph taken at Frederick Ellis May's, a studio in Marlborough Square, Coalville. Soon after, on Friday the 30th October 1914, a wide-eyed Private Sam Boot (1620) marched from Hugglescote to Coalville Station with the rest of the Fifty with a destination of Luton. He was one of the lucky ones who had a spell of Christmas leave. Try to imagine his parent's emotional thoughts as they embraced their son goodbye on the platform in late December 1914, and waved until the train disappeared from view.

On the 1st April 1915 the 5th Leicestershire Battalion took over some shallow, hurriedly dug and particularly dangerous frontline trenches in the Messines Sector of Belgium. The area had been savagely fought over in the autumn of 1914, and putrefying human and animal remains were ubiquitous, and the putrid aroma of death contaminated everyone. The trenches were badly exposed, being situated on the lower slopes of the German held hillock of Spanbroekmolen (Hill 76). Several lads were to lose their lives, invariably by sniping in this unholy of places. The tour (spell of duty) involved four nights, and alternating four days, and it was on the 15th April 1915 that young Sam died. A witness, Private John

George Bennett said that he died instantly when a German sniper's bullet found its target, his head. He was approaching his eighteenth birthday. A friend, almost certainly Cecil Beadman took a photograph of the wooden cross upon his grave and sent it to his parents, and his grave can be seen at Lindenhoek Chalet Military Cemetery, just south of Kemmel.

He was not to lie alone in the soft earth of Flanders for long, soon he had company, and alongside him are other 5th Battalion pals: Walter Allen on the 18th April 1915 (21 years) from Loughborough; Cecil Beadman on the 19th May 1915 (just 21 years) from Hugglescote; Robert Bacchus on the 4th June 1915 (19 years) from Loughborough; Alwyne Baum on the 4th June 1915 (19 years) from Mountsorrel and Harold Blackham on the 4th June 1915 (21years) from Coalville.

From the information I have to hand it appears that Sam Boot was the first of the First Fifty to die in the Great War. I can recall another of the First Fifty, my grandfather Charles Hatter telling me that he could not believe what had happened *'All that training and he never fired his rifle in anger.'*

The Coalville Times of the 30th April 1915, states that Sam was a member of the Coalville Adult School, in which his father was also an official. It continues that on the previous Sunday morning at the School the president, Mr. B.B. Drewett expressed sympathy with the bereaved parents, which the members passed in silence by standing.

Private Ernest Samuel's grave is in Plot 2, Row H, and Grave Number 3 at Lindenhoek Military Cemetery. He lies near to his best pal, Cecil Beadman. Sam's name can be read on the Coalville Clock Tower Memorial, and also on a tablet in St. John The Baptist Church at Hugglescote.

Many thanks to Geoffrey Boot, Sam Boot's nephew for providing identity and information.

Albert Cecil Bradshaw

Always called Cecil, he was born on the 23rd July 1895 at Coalville, the youngest of four brothers of Mr. & Mrs W. F. Bradshaw residing at 5, Gutteridge Street, Coalville. He was educated at the local Wesleyan School on Belvoir Road, and later employed as a blacksmith at Stableford's Wagon Works. Cecil enlisted at Coalville in the third week of August 1914 into the 5th Leicestershire Battalion. He proved to be a very capable soldier and was promoted to lance corporal in 1915 and to a full corporal a year later. Wounded at the storming and capture of the Somme village of Gommecourt in March 1917, he was admitted to hospital in France with a gunshot wound to the knee and suffering from shell shock. Cecil wrote to his parents explaining these details and telling them not to worry, and that he was getting-on as well as could be expected. The Coalville Times of the 24th August 1917, proudly exclaimed that Corporal A. C. Bradshaw, 'One of the Fifty', was at home on leave for the week after being involved in much fighting. (Almost certainly this leave followed his recovery from the earlier wound prior to returning to the front on the St. Elie Left Sector in France).

The Coalville Times of the 2nd February 1918 announced the wedding of Lance-Sergeant Albert Cecil Bradshaw to Miss Florence Trueman, daughter of Mrs. S. Gray of Margaret Street. The wedding took place at Ebenezer Baptist Church on the Ashby Road and Rev. W. H. Wills, who had visited Cecil while he was hospitalised in France, conducted the ceremony. The bride was given-away by her stepfather, Mr. S. Gray

and was attended by two bridesmaids, Miss Evelyn Trueman (sister) and Miss Ethel Maud Bradshaw, sister to the bridegroom. Mr. C. Bradshaw, Cecil's uncle acted as best man. The article concluded by writing that the happy couple received many useful and valuable presents. By this time Cecil was a cadet and scheduled for officer training, however, a delay resulted in his loss of life after three and a quarter years of battling the enemy and the conditions. The brave soldier met his death one month before Armistice Day. He was killed whilst serving as a Lance-Sergeant, still with the 5th Leicestershire Battalion on 11th October 1918. His final battle was in France, close to Riqerval Wood, about twenty-five kilometres (fifteen miles) northeast of St. Quentin. The attack started shortly after midnight and by 5.00 am the Battalion was climbing (in silence) the slopes of a small hill towards the wood. About half way up a few small cottages and thick scrub housed a force of German machine-gunners, and they opened fire. One concealed German showed himself and shot from point blank range, killing many before he was himself killed. The War Diary quotes: *'Among others we lost Sergeants A. C. Bradshaw and W. E. Dimmocks.'* In thirty minutes 'D' Company lost ten killed and fourteen wounded.

The battle raged all day and at 8.00 pm the 5th South Staffordshire relieved the Battalion. Cecil (2551-240631) died at the age of twenty-three, after four years of service.

In July 1915, the Coalville Times announced that all four Bradshaw brothers were serving in the Forces. His eldest brother, Walter H. Bradshaw was born in

1884, a married man and lived at 7, Gutteridge Street. He (Sapper 35102, 42nd Army Troop) had joined the Royal Engineers in March 1915, and he too was a blacksmith at Stableford's Wagon Works. The second brother, Charles. E. Bradshaw was born in 1888, and enlisted at Leicester (29199) in June 1915 into the Royal Artillery as a driver. 'Wag' as he was known was a married man working in Leicester as a baker, and later moved to Broughton Street at Coalville. The couple had five children, Len, Jack, Dorothy, June and one died as a baby.

Most of the veterans attended every Armistice Day Clock Tower Service, and afterwards, 'Wag' and his old pal Edward Fewkes-Griffin (ex-corporal of the 4th (1/4th Leicestershire) toasted their fallen comrades with a large whisky.

The third brother, George F. Bradshaw, born in 1890, was a single pre-war regular soldier. Yet again employed at the Wagon Works, before he was called up on the 4th August 1914 into the Mounted Transport Brigade. In March 1915 he was posted to the Ammunition Column of the Army Service Corps (M2/035274-Corporal-597th M.T. Company A.S.C.). Reports stated that Cecil's wife was absolutely inconsolable, it is uncertain whether she remarried in later life. He was regarded as a very kind-hearted, sincere and pleasant man with a smile for everyone.

Cecil's death was reported in the Coalville Times of 8th November 1918, and his name can be read on the town's Clock Tower Memorial and the war memorial in the Wesleyan Methodist Church, Coalville.

Fred Briers

Fred was born on the 21st November 1892 in a cottage owned by Stableford's Wagon Works on the Mantle

Lane, Coalville. His father worked for the company, and Fred attended the local Belvoir Road School, and later followed his father into employment for the same engineering works. He was the youngest of eleven children, John, Eliza, Tom, Annie, Edwin, Ada, Emma, Clara, Enoch and Millie. The family eventually moved the short distance to 2, Gutteridge Street, close to where a Salvation Army building stands, and almost opposite to where the Bradshaw family lived. He regularly attended Sunday school and the congregation at Ebenezer Baptist Chapel on the Ashby Road. Fred enlisted at Coalville in late August 1914 into the 5th Leicestershire Battalion. He was injured very early in the campaign; a photograph shows him with a walking stick. Following hospital treatment and recovery he was allocated to the 7th Leicestershire Battalion (16025). His name was read out on 23rd April 1915, together with another thirty-eight men who were serving in the Armed Forces.

Fred's daughter, Mary Hall, knows little about his war record: *'I have two postcards from France, one shows a manor house and another showing the ruins at Foncquevillers, near to Gommecourt on the Somme. My father was wounded during the first half of the war and so did not serve the four years at the Front. I also remember old photographs of him sitting alongside Red Cross nurses following his wounding.'* Details reveal that

in 1918 he was an acting-corporal (TR/5/19158 with H Company of the 53rd Y.S B.N. N.F.S.)

Fred married Nellie Baker whilst in his late thirties (related to Walter Baker of the Fifty) and they spent their married life at 186, Ashburton Road in Hugglescote. They had three children, Ted, Mary and Pat. A tall and imposing military figure even after the war, he served in Coalville's Home Guard during World War 2. He was for many years a chief inspector and administrator for Midland Red Buses and later was manager of Coalville's Midland Red Bus Service garage. Fred was a very good friend of Tom Catlow (another of the Fifty), and a bus conductor for the same company. Throughout his life he was a devout Baptist and loved to sing hymns. Fred has been described by two of his relatives as 'a true gentleman.' He died on the 9th January 1986, aged ninety-three years, being cremated. Fred's grandniece, Jane, plays the organ at Ebenezer to this day. Mary states: *'His first words on entering the house were: 'put the kettle on,' but many times I've wished I'd asked him about his life in the military.'*

Many thanks to Mary Hall, and also to Fred's niece, Vera Wilkins (nee Badcock).

Thomas Lord Catlow

Thomas (Tom) was born on the 24th January 1889 at 30, Mantle Lane, Coalville.

He worshipped at and attended Christ Church Bible Class where the highly respected Reverend Hoskins taught, and additionally proved his worth as an excellent footballer, playing for the church team, which won the 1909-10 League. The goalkeeper in that side was Walter Handford, one of the Fifty as was outfielder, Edgar Ewart Boot. After leaving school he became an apprentice blacksmith at Stableford's Wagon Works. Tom, together with several pals enlisted in their hometown into the 5th Leicestershire Battalion. His son, Harold Catlow enthusiastically pointed his father out on the photograph of the Fifty, readers can see him on the extreme left of the rear row. During the course of the war he was badly wounded and discharged from the Army, spending the remainder of the war working in a munitions factory at Nottingham.

Tom married Edith Maud Thirlby at Whitwick Church and their marriage was blessed with two sons, Harold and George.

Following the war employment became very scarce and for Tom, as well as many others, it was a question of taking one temporary job after another.

His fortunes improved when one of his old military pals, Fred Briers, who was a chief inspector on Midland Red Buses, helped to obtain for him the position of a bus conductor. This was typical of the surviving twenty-two members of the Fifty, who for the remainder of their lives did their utmost to support each other during some very difficult times. From 1936 onwards they lived happily at 197, Thornborough Lane, with their children attending the local Bridge Road School. Tom held his job with Midland Red Buses until customary retirement at sixty-five years of age.

Harold said that although his father rarely spoke of his military experiences he remembers his warm friendships with Walter Handford, Jabez Emmerson, Fred Briers and Charles Hatter.

Tom died at Tillson House, an old-folk's home at

Coalville on the 22nd January 1978, having reached the grand age of 88 years.

Harold and his brother were educated at Bridge Road School, and Harold was in the same class as my father, Les Kendrick. Both were excellent athletes and so competition, especially in the hurdling events was very keen. Following school he held a position within the offices of a local coalmine, and his brother, George, managed Bloor's Butchers Shop in Coalville for many years.

During the Second World War, Harold was in the Royal Medical Corps, serving in India and northern Burma at dangerous places such as Imphal and Kohima. He finished the war as an acting Warrant Officer, and married a nurse who he met at Liverpool. Many thanks to Harold Catlow, son of Thomas Catlow.

Christ Church Football Team, League Champions 1909 - 10. Back row; E Hagger, F Storer, W Handford, T Catlow, W Catlow, D Green. Front row; E Hagger, EE Boot, JA Walton, unknown, unknown.

Christ Church Bible Class, 1912. Back row; W Handford, J Farleigh, Rev. S Hosking. Middle row; F Hagger, ... Satchel, T Catlow, JA Walton, AV Brown, CT Walton, W Catlow, D Green. Front row; H Marson, E Hagger, W Aldridge, W Hurst (Teacher), A Storer, EE Boot, F Storer, F Clay.

Cap badge of the Leicestershire Regiment.

Some of the Fifty. Photograph taken in Leopold Street, Loughborough, 1914

Men of the 5th Leicestershire Batallion at Sawbridgeworth, 1914.

Author, Michael Kendrick, with his collection of photographs, letters and artefacts.

Great War silk greetings card.

Church pocket book belonging to Walter Baker, pictured left.

Blood stained birth certificate of son Ernest, recovered from the remains of Charles Cavendish.

Map of the Western Front, 1915

Bullet pendant made by Charles Hatter while in the trenches.

The approximate battle line of the British armies in the west, including the short section in the north from Bixschoote to the sea, held by our Belgian and French allies.

Councillors | **Ambulan**

CHARLES HATTER (centre right) receives the Transport and General Workers' Union gold medal from the Union's Assistant General Secretary (Mr. Harry Nicholas) at the Ex-Servicemen's Club, Coalville, on Friday. Looking on are Mr. Len Robinson (centre left) and Mr. Joe Cox (extreme right). 9962

Transport Union Gives Member A Gold Medal

A GOLD MEDAL, the highest award which the Transport and General Workers' Union can bestow on any of its members, was presented to 63-year-old Mr. Charles Hatter of 180 Central-road, Hugglescote, at a presentation supper at Coalville Ex-Servicemen's Club on Friday night.

The medal, for long and meritorious service, was handed to Mr. Hatter by the Union's Assistant General Secretary, Mr. Harry Nicholas, who was paying his first visit to Coalville.

Village Hall For Copt Oak

COPT OAK Village Hall Committee is to launch an appeal for funds to enable the village hall to be

Great War greetings cards, the one on the left having real sprigs of greenery.

George Bennett seated left, with friends.

Fred Briers, recovering from his injuries.

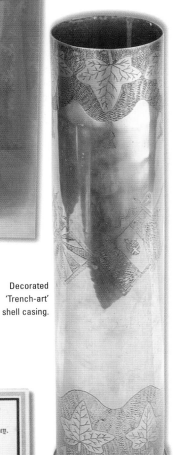

Decorated 'Trench-art' shell casing.

From left: Jabez Emmerson, William Emmerson, Walter Handford, seated - Cyril Crane.

Memorial card to Joseph William Cowley, pictured above.

Laura Gray, great grand-daughter of Charles Hatter in trenches at Vimy Ridge.

Foncquevillers village, Leicester Street Communication Trench ran alongside the church.

Beth Bancroft and Laura Gray in trenches at Sanctuary Wood, 2004.

Gommecourt, looking across the killing field.

The wooden field-cross on Samuel Boot's grave, taken by Cecil Beadman. The gravestone marks his final resting place in Lindenhoek Chalet Military Cemetery.

Charles Cavendish

Charles Cavendish was born on the 14th October 1885, at 21, Crescent Street, Notting Hill, Kensington, London. His father, Alfred, was a marble polisher and his mother's name was Mary (nee Daly). Following a period of retraining as a boilermaker, he applied for a job with Midland Railways to do just that, and being successful the family moved to the Coalville area.

After several years Alfred and Mary felt the pull of the big-city and decided to return to London, however, sixteen years old Charles had other ideas having made many friends and wanted to stay. A solution was found when the Barton family of Baxton's Row of Hugglescote adopted him in 1901. William Barton was forty-three years of age and a coal miner; his wife Georgina, was thirty-six years old. Their niece, Anne, aged four, lived in the household too. Charles was employed as a miner at South Leicestershire Colliery and remained so until 1914. He married Jane James who had lived on Silver Street in Whitwick. The ceremony took place at Ashby de la Zouch Registry Office, and initially they set-up home on Pares Hill at Whitwick. Later they took-up residence at 84, Ashburton Road at Hugglescote. They had five

children, Ernest (Victor Charles Ernest born 1908), Bill, Gordon, Joseph, and the youngest Edward (called Ned).

In late August 1914 Charles, rather than enlisting at Coalville (reason unknown), travelled to Loughborough's Drill Hall to join the 5th Leicestershire Battalion. His grandson, David, proudly points him out on the picture of the Fifty, he can be seen sitting on the second row, third along from the officer with the dog. He served with the Battalion until he was wounded at Ypres, and following a period of recovery was allocated to the 4th (1/4th) Leicestershire Battalion, after their heavy losses at the Battle of Hohenzollern Redoubt. He was again wounded, this time to the head by shrapnel during the Battle of the Somme in July 1916, and was hospitalised for seven weeks. Charles returned home to recuperate and then returned once again to the frontline in France.

Jane Cavendish with sons. From back and left to right: Ernest, Gordon, Joseph, Ned (on knee) and Bill.

Sadly, it was around this time that his wife, Jane, deserted her husband and children. The marriage was dissolved. It is so easy to lay blame, but living during warfare and an uncertain future can play terrible tricks with the mind. A frontline soldier adapts to the hazards of warfare and forges very strong brotherly-bonds, so finding it difficult to come to terms with domestic life at home. These men often felt that by their absence they were letting their friends in the trenches down. Equally, it must have been mentally tortuous for a wife to bring up five young children, knowing that her husband could be killed at any given moment.

Blood-stained birth certificate of son, Ernest, found in a pocket with the remains of Charles Cavendish.

Invariably, in times of crisis good people come to the fore and unmarried Anne, niece to the Barton's who adopted him, brought up three of the children. His youngest child Joseph was brought up at Vicarage Farm, Whitwick by Liz, the sister of Charles's departed wife.

On the 21st October 1917 Charles was wounded yet again, dangerously so in the chest by shrapnel from a bomb dropped by a German aircraft. He was in the St. Elie Left Sector, just to the south of the Hohenzollern Redoubt. He returned to England for hospital treatment, and then rejoined his mates at the frontline in France by March 1918. On June 18th Charles, with others, was gassed on the outskirts of the village of Gorre, and recovered sufficiently to return to his unit. The Battalion was just to the north of Bethune, France, and entrenched within the two villages of Gorre and Essars, which straddled the La Bassee Canal. It was a relatively quiet spot, the weather was characteristically warm and the troops regularly bathed and swam in the cool canal. There was little danger apart from the occasional salvo of shells or an air-attack. After displaying tremendous bravery and determination on several occasions Private Charles Cavendish (241465), was killed on 2nd July 1918. He was victim to a high-explosive shell that killed him instantly. The readers can understand he has no resting place, however, one item found in the remains of his jacket pocket was a bloodstained certificate of registry of birth for his eldest son; Victor Charles Ernest Cavendish. No explanation can be offered why he was carrying this on his person. Such are the fortunes of war (and life).

Charles was thirty-two years of age and his name is commemorated on Pane 42/44 at the Loos Memorial, and also can be read on the Coalville Clock Tower Memorial.

Strangely, none of Charles's family can ever recall receiving the medals that he so richly deserved. This anomaly has recently been corrected by David.

Many thanks to a good friend, David Cavendish, who is the son of Joseph. David also possesses his grandfather's military bible. On several occasions we have spoken of the bravery and determination of Charles on the military front, but he also had to contend with the death of his parents and the desertion of his wife.

Arthur Congrave

Arthur was born in 1897 at Ravenstone, the son of Mr & Mrs Thomas Congrave, and indeed apart from the war spent most of his life in the village at 29, Wash Lane. He was the middle-born of three brothers and he also had three sisters. His brothers were Harold (born 1896), Eric (born 1900) and sisters Alice, Aggie and Ida.

He attended Ravenstone Parish Church and was a good friend of Harry Walker, another of the Fifty. Upon leaving school he obtained employment at Stableford's Wagon Works in Coalville. Arthur, a tall man with a kindly disposition enlisted at Coalville in the first week of the war into the 5th Leicestershire Battalion, aged 17. The Coalville Times of the 16th July 1915 printed a letter Arthur sent to his parents (written on the 2nd July) regarding the death of Harry Walker.

' I am quite well and I am writing today because I do not think I will have a chance tomorrow. We had a very heavy shelling last night but I am pleased to say that little damage was done to our trenches, but I am sorry to say that Harry Walker got killed. He was shot at six this morning and died almost straight away, thus suffering no pain. It will put his mother about, especially, but he died for his country. I am going to write to Mr Dowling today to let him know. I expect

you may have heard of the honour our regiment has won out here. We are now the Royal Leicestershire Regiment. Come on the Tigers. The Germans don't like the Leicesters at all, and threaten to pull our tail, but it is the other way about. They haven't pulled the Tiger's tail yet and they don't look like doing so.'

In the letter to the Rev. Dowling (Rector of Ravenstone Church) he wrote that he and William Kendrick had buried Harry Walker on the 2nd July 1915 near to where he fell. He asked the Reverend to convey their sincere sympathies to the Walker family. William Kendrick, who survived the war, was also born on Wash Lane and grew-up with the two aforementioned. In August 1916, Arthur (2545) was badly wounded at Monchy au Bois in France, and had to have his right leg amputated, and for anything other than short journeys he used an invalid carriage. Whilst in hospital in France his mother travelled to visit him, he was later transferred to a hospital at Edmonton. For many years Arthur kept on his mantelpiece the jagged piece of shell casement, that had ripped into his upper thigh and which caused him so much pain and anguish.

Arthur happily married Emma Bentley, the daughter of Ely Bentley, a local farmer, and they had four children, unfortunately one daughter (Janet) was to die tragically in a house fire.

Arthur's elder brother, Harold, formerly a miner at Snibston Colliery was in the 7th Battalion of the Leicestershire Regiment (203429) and was killed on the 19th September 1918 during an attack against Epehy, near Cambrai in France. He was a member of the Parish Church choir and assistant scoutmaster of the Ravenstone Troop. The Coalville Times of the 16th October 1918 reported the death of the twenty-one year old, also Arthur being one of the Famous Fifty and his leg-amputation, and that of young Eric training with the army in England.

Arthur spent most of his working life in the Lamp Cabin at Snibston Colliery, where another of the Fifty, namely Jabez Emmerson, was the manager. When shifts permitted he and his wife did the caretaking duties at Snibston School, where Leicestershire's War Poet, Arthur Newberry Choyce was the headmaster. Arthur and Eric (who lived with his wife, Evelyn at 29, Wash Lane) were both members of St. John Ambulance Brigade.

Arthur's grandson, Philip Alldread, son of Roy Alldread and Mary (nee Congrave), lives in Coalville, and remembers with great affection: *'Granddad and grandma regularly visited my wife and I on a Sunday night. He also enjoyed a game of dominoes and cards at the Marlborough Club, Coalville and the Plough at Ravenstone. He loved watching cricket and golf, and for about forty years took his holidays at the Winslow Hotel on Hull Road, Blackpool. (See photograph). Granddad spoke quietly but fairly quickly, he was a good man.'*

Arthur died in 1970, not long after the death of his daughter, Mary, and lies buried in Ravenstone Churchyard. His wife, Emma followed in September 1983. Harold's name can be read on Ravenstone's War Memorial that sits in the church grounds. Many thanks to Arthur's niece, Mrs Pollard, the daughter of Alice Congrave and also to an old friend of Arthur's, Jim Smith. Special thanks to Arthur's grandson, Phillip Alldread.

Joseph William Cowley

Joseph (mostly called Bill - and I will use this name) was born in 1896. He was the eldest son of two brothers and six sisters of Joseph and Eliza Cowley who lived at 57, North Street in Hugglescote (later renumbered 182, Central Road). Joseph (senior) was an exceptional euphonium player with the Hugglescote and Ellistown Silver Band, and was regarded in high-circles as possibly the finest in England, and young Bill played tenor-horn for the same band.

Later the family moved the short distance to 118,

Central Road in the same village, and it was there that the family lived for many years. (After the war my grandparents lived for nearly fifty years at 180, Central Road).

Naturally, with coming from a musical family Bill was a chorister at St. John The Baptist Church, Grange Road in the village and also attended the local Church School. (Which still stands on the corner of Station Road). Upon leaving school he followed the traditional route of many of his friends and became a miner, working for a spell at South Leicestershire Colliery before moving to Stableford's Wagon Works as a blacksmith's striker. Later his mining skills were to be put to use beneath the battlefields of the Great War.

Bill Cowley, along with old school chums Charles Hatter, Bill Massey and Cecil Beadman were among the early volunteers at Coalville into the 5th Leicestershire Battalion.

In the spring of 1915 the Battalion was in the Messines Sector of Belgium, with their frontline trenches on the slopes of Spanbroekmolen Hill. Amongst other dangers 'tunnel-mining' was a serious problem. The Germans were digging and detonating high explosives beneath our lines. Lieutenant Aubrey Moore, a qualified mine surveyor asked for volunteers to form a counter-tunnelling section. Twenty-four men volunteered. Primarily they had a mining background and along with Bill were Jabez and William Emmerson of Bagworth, Cecil Hurley of Donisthorpe, William Barney of Ellistown, and Bill Toon and Harry Starbuck from Appleby Magna. This tunnelling-party was superb, brilliantly led and demonstrated immense bravery time and again. They spent many hours working underground, often only a few yards from enemy sappers. Soon after the creation of this party they detected two enemy mineshafts being worked and destroyed them with a camouflet. Shortly afterwards the 5th Leicestershire moved into the perilous Ypres Salient, where their outstanding troglodytic work continued. It was never possible to detect all of the

enemy mines, and on the evening of the 23rd July 1915 one devastated a huge section of the Battalion's frontline. Many died instantly, some suffocated under mounds of earth and casualties were heavy. Precisely one week later on the 30th July 1915, Corporal Emmerson and Private Starbuck displayed tremendous courage and personal confidence when discovering another mine. The pair observed that everything was primed and could be blown-up at any given time. Without hesitation they quickly cut the detonator-wires and half a ton of Westphalite was removed. Such outstanding action saved the lives of many of their comrades; the gallant pair being awarded D.C.M.s (Distinguished Conduct Medals). Cecil Hurley was to receive the same decoration for selfless courage underground. Tunnelling was and is an exceptionally dangerous job in any theatre of war, and an excellent book entitled, 'Birdsong' by Sebastian Foulkes, gives an indication and an insight into the hazards involved. As mentioned earlier, mines were also planted with the sole intention of killing opposing sappers.

When accidentally disturbing enemy shafts, confrontations often resulted in fierce hand-to-hand fighting to the death. The bravery and sacrifice of these men cannot be over-emphasised, and great credit must go to the officer who led from the front, Lieutenant (later Captain) Aubrey Moore, the son of the rector of Appleby Magna.

The 46th North Midland Division entrained in October 1915 to fight in one of the most ferocious battles of the war, namely the charge of the

Hohenzollern Redoubt. It was situated just to the north of Loos in northern France. For two long days and nights our lads battled against gas, heavy-shelling, hand-to-hand fighting, murderous machine gun fire with no sleep, and little food or water. The 4th (1/4th) Battalion was decimated and the 5th (1/5th) suffered terribly also.

During February 1916 the Battalions were in another bitterly contested area, Vimy Ridge, just south of Arras in France, where tunnel-mining was all too common. To this day massive craters remain to remind visitors where huge mines were detonated; in places the craters (and the opposing troops that occupied them) are only metres apart. During tunnelling the subsoil was removed by bagging-it and distributing it well behind the frontline, so avoiding the enemy's suspicion. It was laborious and dangerous work and on the night of the 7th and 8th May 1916 the enemy blew a counter-mine close to where four men of 'D' Company had been working. Two of the men were never seen again. The other two, bruised and badly shaken crawled out of the shaft in a half-naked condition. The next day the 9th May, the Battalions moved southwards to the old village of Lucheux. Here they regrouped, refitted and rested prior to rehearsals for the attack which was to commence on the 1st July 1916, namely the Battle of the Somme.

Prior to this period British tunnellers had been very active in the Somme region, preparing several enormous mines that were to be exploded concurrently on that opening day. Later a similar operation was to apply in the area of the Messines Ridge in Belgium. Private William Cowley (2560) was killed on the 8th May 1916, aged just 20 years. His name is remembered on the Thiepval Memorial, Somme, in France.

There has always been something of a mystery as to where Bill actually died.

Bill's body was never found, so almost certainly he was one of the tunnellers who died on the night of 7/8th May at Vimy Ridge. If so why is his name etched

on Thiepval Memorial (Somme), some thirty kilometres (twenty miles) to the south?

On the 9th May the 5th Battalion moved to Lucheux, about twenty-five kilometres (fifteen miles) from where the 5th attacked at Gommecourt on the opening day of the Battle of the Somme.

Could Bill have been released to help the Tunnelling Companies of the Royal Engineers on the Somme? If so why is he registered as dying with the 5th Leicestershire Battalion? Also, by 1916 the Army had enlisted many colliers to undertake tunnel mining, and Bill would have been needed at Vimy. I believe that Bill was one of the two men who perished when the German's blew a mine. Perhaps administration played a part in this mystery and his death was not registered until arriving at Lucheux.

Joseph and Eliza Cowley received a letter on the 19th May 1916 informing them of Bill's death. The Coalville Times released the news a

few days later and expressed sorrow at the 'Loss of another of the Fifty. He was a very popular young man.'

His mother especially was shattered by the news.

Joseph and Eliza Cowley

Her youngest son, John (Jack) said: 'Not only have I lost a brother, but also my hero.' For weeks his father was stunned, in a dream world, and often to be seen smoking his pipe, deep in melancholy thought. Joseph lived into his nineties and shortly before his death a newspaper account informed readers that he could remember Hugglescote Parish Church being built, and how the first oil lamp was an improvement on candles for household use.

Before the war Bill was very close to his girlfriend, Ivy York. It was felt that only the circumstances were delaying marriage, and she too was inconsolable. Ivy remained friends of the family for the remainder of her life, often discussing of what might have been. One of Bill's sisters, Nellie Reynolds married and owned a shop that once existed at the bottom of Breach Road, on the corner of Forest Road, Hugglescote. Jack's son, John Cowley kept up the military tradition by being a regular in the Grenadier Guards, and his son, Jason is invariably in charge of the Ashby Remembrance Day parade.

Bill is remembered on the town's Clock Tower Memorial, and also on a tablet in St. John The Baptist Church at Hugglescote.

Shortly after Bill's death, on Empire Day, the Church School's flag was set at half-mast in his memory. Bill knew of the risks involved, yet was prepared to sacrifice his life for the future well being of our country. God bless him and all like him, especially on Remembrance Day.

Many thanks to local man, John Cowley, nephew to Bill.

Henry Cramp

Henry was born in the 1890s and was the son of John Cramp. Little is known of him apart from he managed his father's hairdressing business at Ellistown. He enlisted at Coalville in mid-August into the 5th Leicestershire Battalion. In the Coalville Times of the 29th June 1917, it announced that he had earlier received wounds whilst fighting with the 5th Battalion in France. It continued that after recovery Henry was posted to another unit fighting in the Salonica Campaign (Balkans) against the Bulgarians. He was subsequently wounded again and was hospitalised in Malta. The article proudly stated that: 'He was one of the first fifty volunteers.' Henry survived the war, but not so for his assistant, John Callier (not Collier) who worked in the hairdressing shop. He was a twenty-one year old lance corporal (22469) in the 2nd Leicestershire Battalion when he was killed on the 23rd April 1917 in Mesopotamia. John, an Ashby de la Zouch man, was living at Ibstock and was a Sunday school teacher at the Wesleyan School in the village.

Charles Dedman

I remember a conversation with my grandfather who was smiling and informing me that there was a 'Deadman' in the Fifty.

'Charley' was born in 1887, one of four sons of Charley and Emma Dedman of Hand Terrace, Sawbridgeworth in Hertfordshire. No trace can be found of his decision to move to northwest Leicestershire, however he worked for a Mr. R. Tebbett, a saddler on Hotel Street, Coalville from 1904-14, and during this time had lived at nearby Swannington. Charley (2450) enlisted at Coalville in the first week of the war into the 5th Leicestershire Battalion. It is ironical that for several weeks of his military training he was based in the town of his birth. I can only assume he was wounded and reposted, because little is known until his death. Charley received a bullet to the head whilst serving as a rifleman with the 13th Kensington (County of London, Princess Louise's Battalion), the London Regiment. His battalion reported him missing on the 9th September 1916, and he was laid to rest at Guillemont Road Cemetery, Guillemont, on the Somme. (Revised service number 7948). The Commonwealth War Graves Commission gives his age as twenty-nine years, however local press reported his age as twenty-six. A friend in Swannington received a letter from a French soldier, Clesse Noel, who sympathetically wrote that Charley had been struck in the head by a German bullet, from which he died. He added that he was buried two hundred yards northeast of (censored), and that he found the Swannington address on a photograph lying near to his body. 'He must have been looking at it in his last moments. A lot of friends attended his burial and the grave is marked by a little wooden cross.'

The Swannington address also received a letter from his sergeant major informing the recipient that he knew Dedman to be: 'A good comrade and a keen and reliable soldier, his loss is greatly regretted by all in the London Regiment.'

The Coalville Times of the 17th November 1916

confirmed his death and wrote that his mother still resided in Sawbridgeworth, and that she still had three other sons fighting in the Forces.

It is possible that Charley's name is on the Kensington Memorial at the junction of Church Street and Kensington High Street.

His name can be read on the War Memorial Plaque in Swannington Church (spelt Deadman).

Many thanks to Lesley Hale of the Whitwick Historical Group for the above information.

Jabez Emmerson. D.C.M. & William Henry Emmerson

Private Jabez Emmerson. 5th Leicestershire. 1914.

William Emmerson, the 'Grand Master' playing for Nottinghamshire in 1959.

Both Jabez and William were born in Bagworth, a small mining village five kilometres (three miles) southeast of Coalville. They were two of the three sons of Alfred Barratt Emmerson. Jabez was second-born on the 27th July 1894 and William on the 6th December 1888.

Within this area of Leicestershire the name of Emmerson has for over a century been synonymous with bravery, intelligence and success. Initially the surname was connected with several local collieries, however, during the Great War of 1914-18 heroism and sacrifice embroidered the name even more so.

Many readers will be familiar with Leicestershire's worst mining disaster at Whitwick Colliery on the 19th April 1898. A total of thirty-five colliers died and only seven survived. One of the rescue team that battled so valiantly was the same Alfred Barratt Emmerson. He was born in 1856 at Abersychan, Monmouthshire, and started to work down the mines at the age of fourteen. Highly intelligent he went to Mining College at Sheffield and took up a position at Cannock Chase. Whilst there an underground explosion trapped him, so he was fully aware of all the dangers involved in rescue attempts. Alfred held senior positions in both Yorkshire and Derbyshire before becoming manager of Bagworth Colliery, and finally at nearby Ellistown. He stayed at the latter colliery for twenty-nine years until his retirement in 1926, dying in 1940. Alfred and his wife were committed and respected members of the local Wesleyan Methodist Church. Jabez and William studied at Ashby de la Zouch Grammar School, Jabez being a contemporary of Aubrey Moore, who is regularly mentioned in this book. The two daughters,

Standing from left: Boam, J Emmerson, Beardmore. Seated from left: Hallam, W Handford, Neal. 5th Leicestershire, Christmas 1915.

carriage, very cold. Left port at 9.30 pm on 'Atalanta', had to return after ten hours, sea too rough. Seasick. No sleep. 27th February: left port again at 8.00 pm. Seasick. No sleep. Arrived at Le Havre the following day.'

The diary continues by explaining the terrible conditions at the front, the severe cold, the endurance training, and casualties. 6th March 1915: 'On sentry duty all day. We lost Ernie Porter today and Corporal Green was injured in the back. 8th March 1915: Just cooked bacon breakfast, very cold and frosty night. We are 500 yards from enemy trenches. 11th March 1915: Rotten sanitary conditions. Slept with greatcoat on. Big guns firing. March 13th 1915: On parade at 5.30am. Saw Alf and Joe* in the afternoon. 21st March 1915: Church service conducted by Colonel Jones. William, Walter and Cyril spending day in Bailleul. 10th April 1915: Had to leave William and friends for first time, now under Lieutenant Aubrey Moore. 12th April 1915: threw some bombs today. Saw Alf and Joe at a neighbouring barn and we had a chat and a sing. 25th April 1915: Bomb throwing and hear that Henry Chapman has been killed. Writing letters. 10th May 1915: Heard the lark whistling. Enemy attacked 4th Leicestershire but was repulsed, caused great commotion.

Maggie and Helen (Nellie) were educated at a 'Dame' School where they were taught music, dressmaking and advanced cookery. The two sons followed in their father's footsteps, passing surveying examinations and working at Snibston, Mapperley and Swanwick Collieries.

William and Jabez enlisted at Coalville in mid-August into the 5th Leicestershire Battalion, the two signing the dotted line just ahead of Charles Hatter (2534) and Frederick Hart (2535). In February 1915 the Battalion landed at Le Havre, France. Jabez (2532) was in No. 8 Platoon, 'C' Company and quickly received promotion to Lance Corporal. In 1915 his diary contains home addresses of friends within the battalion who were to perish at a later date. John Burnham of Mountsorrel and Clifford (Jas) Scott of Ellistown being two of them.

William and his wife, Jabez and his fianceé, parents and grandparents. Ellistown, circa 1917.

The 1915 Diary of Jabez Emmerson.

Early entries into the diary: '24th January 1915: Played organ whilst at home on leave. 25th February 1915: Left Sawbridgeworth at midnight by train. 26th February: Arrived at Southampton 9.00 am. Eight of us per

14th May 1915: Taken by motorbus to Ypres and then marched to trenches. We are between Ypres and Hill 60. Hot spot. Dead soldiers lying all around place, shells coming from all directions. Back with William and Walter. 17th May 1915: Very busy day. Captain Chapman and Lieutenant Selwyn are badly wounded.

William, his wife and their son Eric. Ellistown, circa 1917.

May 18th 1915: Lieutenant Selwyn has died. Don't hold out much hope for Captain Chapman. June 5th 1915: Hear Captain Chapman has died. 29th June 1915: In trenches between Hill 60 and Zillebeke. Hot place. 27th July 1915: My 21st Birthday - in trenches.' It continued with the months at Ypres, then gradually thins out to the extent whereby the appalling battle of Hohenzollern Redoubt on October 13th 1915, is simply mentioned, with no description given. *'Too busy, too grim.'*

*Alf and Joe mentioned above were cousins. Walter is Walter Handford. Cyril is Cyril Crane.

Lieutenant Aubrey Moore, an old school friend from Appleby Magna, had set up a 'tunnelling company' for counter-mining purposes on the Messines' battlefront (spring 1915). Jabez, a qualified mining surveyor naturally played a key role. Aubrey Moore recalls: *'We had driven under the German line and kept a man there listening for any enemy offensive action. One Sunday evening I went to the end and found Jabez there with a prayer book in his hand. He told me that his people would now be in chapel and that he wanted to participate from a distance. We were ten feet below a German trench packed with troops, and I remember thinking how odd and yet how devout he was.'*

It was shortly afterwards on 30th July 1915, that Corporal Jabez Emmerson and Private Starbuck received Distinguished Conduct Medals for outstanding bravery. They received the award for dismantling an enemy mine, thus saving the lives of scores of men. (There is no mention in his diary of receiving this prestigious award).

The Coalville Times of the 4th February 1916 reveals the award for Corporal Jabez Emmerson. It also mentions that Lance Corporal William Emmerson had resigned his position of surveyor at Swanwick Colliery, Derbyshire, to become one of the First Fifty, and how too he was in the tunnelling team. Jabez continued to demonstrate great leadership qualities and was promoted to sergeant. He was selected as an officer cadet and sent for officer training to Scotland in July 1916. On the 25th October 1916 he was commissioned and transferred to the 7th Leicestershire Battalion. The Coalville Times of the 19th October 1917 stated that Jabez had been admitted into hospital in France with severe gunshot wounds to the leg. He participated in some of the worst conflicts of the war and possessed outstanding leadership qualities.

On the 26th September 1918 Captain J. Emmerson married his fiancée, Bertha Black.

After the war he returned to Coalville and continued as a mining surveyor until 1924, when he became manager of Snibston Colliery. Happily married he lived at 56, Vaughan Street, Coalville and his son,

From rear: Sgt. Hancroft, 4th Leicstershires, Sgt. Shosbroe, 1st Kensingtons, Gnr. Archer, London Yeomanry, Sgt. Jabez Emmerson, 5th Leicestershires, Pte. Tom Purdley, 1st Monmouth's. Aux-le-Chateau, 1916.

From rear; Lance-Corporal Shannon, Corporal Freestone, Corporal Ladkin, Sergeant Faulks, Company Sergeant Major Wood, Captain Jabez Emmerson, Company Qtr. Master Sergeant Major Ringoose, Sergeant James. 7th Leicestershire Battalion N.C.O's, Louth, January 1919.

Philip and daughter Jean, were born there.

A popular sportsman and like his father he adored cricket, and captained the Snibston First Eleven from 1924-34, winning the Coalville Times Cup in 1928. He was also a senior figure in 'Toc-H' circles (Skipper Emmerson), and remained an excellent comrade to survivors of the First Fifty, especially to Walter Handford and Charles Hatter. Indeed whilst Jabez was a Justice of the Peace, he asked my grandfather to apply to become a J.P. (He kindly refused the offer on the grounds that he had no wish to judge his fellow man).

Bertha Emmerson.

Jabez moved to 157, Broom Leys Road and it was from there that he bitterly criticised the Germans (Nazis) in the Thirties and during World War 2. His dear wife died in 1947 at the age of fifty-four years from a sudden brain haemorrhage, and he later remarried. Jabez and Walter Handford remained great friends, and would spend hours drinking tea and chatting about 'the old days' after service at St. David's Church. Jabez died on the 1st April 1980, and his ashes lie close to Walter's in St. David's Garden of Remembrance. I believe that Jabez was the last of the First Fifty to pass-on. In many respects a great man who achieved notable success in his long life.

As a fitting tribute I would like readers to remember that it was Captain Jabez Emmerson

D.C.M. who contacted the surviving members of the Fifty, and they rightly led the procession for the unveiling of Coalville's Clock Tower Memorial on the 31st October 1925 in front of a crowd of ten thousand people.

William Emmerson used all of his surveying knowledge and skills as a tunneller alongside Jabez in the early stages of the war. He fought in the Battle of Hohenzollern, surviving unscathed. However, within a few days he was suffering from severe stomach cramps, and was sent to Cambridge Hospital for treatment (appendix removed). He quietly won promotion to Quarter Master Sergeant and remained with the 5th Leicestershire for the full four years.

I have read a touching letter addressed to his father on 14th February 1915. It was sent from

Jabez in 1955, aged 61.

Sawbridgeworth and he writes that Jabez travelled to Luton the day before to complete a shooting course. He then hoped that his father liked the photograph of himself, Jabez, Walter Handford and Cyril Crane. (Included in the colour section). William married Louie Alton (born 20-11-1889) just before he embarked for France. His wife gave birth to a son, Eric, during the conflict.

After the war, William returned to the position that had been retained for him, that of a mining surveyor at Swanick Colliery, Derbyshire. He enjoyed most sports, especially playing and watching tennis and cricket.

During World War Two he was Head Warden for Riddings, about three kilometres from Swanwick. (Derby was bombed during the war). By 1948 he held the position of senior surveyor and was responsible for six local pits. He keenly enjoyed the game of chess and played regularly for Nottinghamshire County Team. William, quieter than his brother, yet equally intelligent died on the 22nd March 1973.

Many thanks to Jabez's son, Philip (sadly deceased) and his wife, Norma. The same gratitude to William's son, Eric, and Alfred Emmerson's granddaughter, Blanche Wyatt.

Francis Glynn

'Frank' resided at 119, North Street at Whitwick. Little is known of him apart that following school he was employed as a miner at a local colliery. He enlisted at Coalville in mid-August into the 5th Leicestershire Battalion, 'D' Company. At the outbreak of the war he was working at Stableford's Wagon Works, Coalville. The Coalville Times of the 15th January 1915 prints a *'Stableford's Roll of Honour'*, listing the names of seventy-three ex-employees now serving with the King's Forces.

During his spell with the 5th Battalion, Frank (2527) utilised his mining experience as part of Lieutenant Aubrey Moore's Tunnelling Section. I have no details to confirm my opinion but it appears that his abilities were sought after, because he was subsequently transferred and completed the war as Sapper F. Glynn (WR/179208) with the Royal Engineers. Frank survived the war.

Walter Gray

Walter Gray (centre) at Ebenezer Bible Class in 1913. William Goacher is to his left and George Holmes to his right.

Walter was born at Hugglescote in 1894. He was the son of Mr & Mrs. Samuel Gray who later moved to Margaret Street at Coalville. He was educated at St. John The Baptist Church School at Hugglescote and the Wesleyan Belvoir Road School, and was a regular attendee at Ebenezer Baptist Bible Class. Amongst his good friends were Fred Briers, Walter Baker, Victor Woolley, George Bennett and John Williamson.

Following school he was employed as a driller at Stableford's Wagon Works.

At the time of his enlistment at Coalville in mid-August into the 5th Leicestershire Battalion, he and his brother, James were living at his Auntie Gray's house, 183, Belvoir Road, Coalville.

A wide-eyed sincere man with a deep-faith, he was extremely popular about town, and many were upset to hear and later read of the manner of his death.

Victor Woolley, one of the Fifty wrote from the trenches to inform Mr & Mrs Gray of their son's death. A letter from Lichfield Territorial Office confirmed it. Private Walter Gray (2528) died on the evening of the 23rd July 1915, when the Germans blew a mine under Trench 50, close to Hill 60, in the Ypres Salient.

The Coalville Times of the 24th September 1915 chronicled Walter's death.

The Commander of 'B' Company, 5th Leicestershire Battalion, Captain J. G. Griffiths wrote the following letter on the 27th July 1915.

'I have to write to tell you of the loss of your son, Pte. W. Gray on Friday last when the enemy exploded a mine immediately under our trench where your son was. Every search has been made for him, but unfortunately we have not been able to find him, nor will we. We shall erect a cross to his memory at the spot where the explosion occurred.

Your son was much liked by his officers and comrades and he was always a good and cheerful worker and he will be much missed. Kindly accept my sympathy and also that of the whole Company in your sad bereavement.

Yours sincerely, J. G. Griffiths. (Captain).'

Walter's body was never found, but as you have read earlier he rests in good company with several of his dear friends and comrades. He is remembered on the Menin Gate War Memorial in Ypres, Belgium. Walter's name can be read on Ebenezer Chapel's Roll of Honour, on a tablet in St. John The Baptist Church, Hugglescote, and on the Coalville Clock Tower Memorial. He was a mere twenty years of age.

The aforementioned brother, James Herbert Gray became a lance corporal with the 512th H.S. Employment Company (164963), surviving the war.

Isaac Hall

Isaac was born at Thringstone in 1896. He was the son of Mr & Mrs John Hall who resided on John Henson's Lane in the village. The local press states that John was a popular figure at the Whitwick Imperial football matches. Isaac and his brother Ernest worshipped at the Parish Church of St. Andrews, Thringstone. Following school he was employed as a miner at Whitwick Colliery, where his elder brother, Ernest also worked on the coalface. Ernest had been a regular soldier with the Tiger's Regiment and at the outbreak of war was a reservist for the 2nd Battalion. He was called up and was one of the British Expeditionary Force of one hundred thousand soldiers. Ernest was married to Anna (nee Bennett) who was the elder sister of George Harry Bennett, another of the First Fifty.

Isaac Hall enlisted at Coalville in the first week of the war into the 5th Leicestershire Battalion. He was seventeen years old. Shortly after arriving in France in late February 1915, and being within several kilometres of where his brother had been fighting, he heard that Ernest had been killed on the 13th March 1915. Ernest (12041) perished at the Battle of Neuve Chappelle, France. He was in the same battalion as one of Leicestershire's finest sons, Private W. Buckingham V.C. who was decorated in this battle for rendering aid to the wounded whilst exposed to heavy fire.

The Coalville Times of the 26th February 1915 released a letter sent to his wife, whereby he wrote the weather had been bitterly cold but now he was in 'a hot spot,' but that it is all in a good cause. The same newspaper on the 5th April 1915 confirmed his death, and wrote that he was the first Whitwick soldier (he was living there pre-war) to be killed in the war.

Isaac sent a letter to his parents shortly before his death:

'Dear Mum and Dad,

Thank you for your letter and parcel and copy of the Coalville Times.

I'm very pleased with all the contents. I'm writing from the trenches, the second night of our tour. It's a bit rough - rained all night. I often think of dear old home but I've got to stick it. I'm in the pink, and I'll come home and see you one of these fine days. I don't think the war will last much longer. Your loving son, Isaac.'

Isaac (2521) met his death at the same time as Walter Gray and George Andrews on the 23rd July 1915. He was aged eighteen years. A German mine exploded under trench 50 close to Hill 60, in the Ypres Sector.

Fortunately Isaac's body was located in that melee of death and destruction and he is buried at Sanctuary Wood Cemetery, close to where he fell in the Ypres Salient, Belgium.

The names of Ernest and Isaac Hall can be read on the War Memorial in St. Andrew's Church.

James Horace Hall

James was born in Whitwick in 1895. Mr. H. T. Bastard at the Whitwick Church School taught him in his early years. He was also a member of the Wesleyan Church on Belvoir Road, and of Mr T. Frith's Bible Class. He lived with his parents and was the only son of Mr and Mrs James Hall at 86, Belvoir Road, Coalville. After leaving school he was employed at Stableford's Wagon Works, where his father also had employment.

He enlisted at Coalville in mid-August 1914 into the 5th Leicestershire Battalion and was wounded in Belgium. Later he was sent home with 'trench feet'. Upon recovery he was reposted to the 1st Leicestershire Battalion and on October 14th 1917 sent a field card home stating that he was quite well. He was delighted because he had just been promoted to lance corporal. A letter received on Monday 29th October 1917

informed his parents that their only son was killed in action on the 15th October 1917. He was killed in the Loos Sector of France.

The Coalville Times of the 2nd November 1917 notified readers of the death of another of the Fifty. James's name can be read on the tablet at the Wesleyan Church and also on the Coalville Clock Tower Memorial.

Walter Handford

Walter was born on the 28th August 1893 to Mr & Mrs W. Handford of Wigston, once a village now a suburb eight kilometres (five miles) southeast of Leicester City centre. His parents took him as a toddler to 95, Highfield Street, Coalville. His father moved there shortly after locating employment in the area. He had a brother, Ernest, about ten years older than himself, and he received his early education at the local Wesleyan School on Belvoir Road. A quietly spoken boy of considerable ability, especially in a musical direction, and yet was modest and never one to push himself. The earliest photograph of Walter shows him as goalkeeper for Christ Church (Coalville) Football League Team, Champions 1909-10. Two other members of the team were also in the Fifty, namely Thomas Catlow and Edgar Boot. The second photograph shows him as a member of Christ Church Bible Class in 1912. Walter and his mother had life-long friendships with the resident vicar, Reverend Hoskins. (See Thomas Catlow photograph).

Walter's daughter, Joyce has recalled many aspects of his life.

'Father was a quiet man and never liked to have his photograph taken. His first love was his family but his second was undoubtedly music, especially the organ. Pop first played in public when he was very young, either ten or eleven. It was at St. Faiths Church, at the top of Highfield Street, opposite to the end of Crescent Road

(where my granny lived). The organist failed to arrive due to illness, and so granny pushed Pop forward, and from that day onwards he continued to play until the age of seventy-five years. The vicar at that time was, Reverend Wallace, who also looked after Ravenstone Church; and he was a lovely, saintly man. Pop was a gifted musician and granny made sure he had the necessary qualifications. He was a medallist from the Victoria College of Music and he was particularly noted for his ability to play classical and sacred music with great eloquence.

The Wedding Day, 15th March 1918. St. John The Baptist, Hugglescote.

Upon leaving college he became music-master at Ashby Boys' High School, also the choirmaster and organist for St. Helen's Church, Ashby. Additionally he was a member of the local philharmonic society, and it was here that he was to meet my mother, Nellie Chambers. She had a lovely singing voice and Pop used to accompany her for presentations.'

The 4th August 1914, along came the war and Walter was among the first to enlist. He was already friendly with the confident, outgoing Jabez Emmerson and that friendship continued for the remainder of his

Walter Handford, 1893 - 1977 with friend Jabez Emmerson 1894 - 1980, (left). The last photograph taken at the home of Jabez in 1972.

The Coalville Times of the 15th March 1918 described the wedding: *'The bride, Nellie Chambers, daughter of former Leicestershire miner's agent Thomas Chambers and his wife (of Belvoir Road) was given away by her father. Nellie wore a crepe de chine dress trimmed with silver lace, with a wreath of orange blossom and veil, and carried a sheaf of white lilies. There were three bridesmaids, Miss Fanny Price of Coalville and Miss M. Parsons of Hugglescote wore pink crepe de chine and black picture hats, and Miss Gladys Hunt (niece of the bride). The latter was also attired in pink crepe de chine with a hat to match and carried a sheaf of lilies and narcissi. Mr. Ernest Handford (brother of the bridegroom) acted as best man. Canon Broughton performed the ceremony in the presence of a good congregation. Both the bride and bridegroom are well known in Coalville and Ashby musical circles, the bride being a talented singer and popular at concerts in the district. The bridegroom, before the war, occupied the position of organist at the Ashby Parish Church, and was a well-known music teacher. He is one of the Famous Fifty (2518) and has subsequently been commissioned by the Leicestershire Regiment.'*

life. Indeed in Jabez's 1915 War Diary he often referred to his pal, Walter.

Joyce continues, *'I can see the pair sitting at St. David's Church, Broomleys, and then crossing the road to where Jabez lived for a cup of coffee and a chat about World War One.'*

They were both in the 5th Leicestershire Battalion and their ability was to show through with early promotions. Walter was a trusted and respected non-commissioned officer with the Battalion. The Coalville Times of the 7th January 1916 proudly reported that Walter Handford, one of the 'Famous Fifty' had been in Coalville during the week; he was on leave from France. In the same newspaper of the 11th August 1916 it states that he been wounded, no other details. Promotions followed and he was selected as an officer cadet.

He returned home for a spell of leave at the end of 1917 before passing on to Trinity College, Cambridge for Officer Training. Before returning to the battlefields he married his 'singing partner' on the 12th March 1918, at St. John The Baptist, Hugglescote.

'Mother said it was a wonderful horse-and-carriage wedding, and she was so proud of her husband in his brand new officer's uniform. They spent a honeymoon at the 'Blue Boar' in Trumpington Street, straight opposite to Trinity College. I have stayed there several times myself, and always think of my parents.'

Walter returned to the frontlines to take his place initially as a 2nd Lieutenant with the 9th Leicestershire Battalion of the 110th Brigade, Leicestershire Regiment. However, heavy losses meant a reorganisation and he became an officer in the 8th Battalion, quickly being involved in some momentous battles trying to stem the German Spring Offensives. (As described earlier involving James Bancroft).

On the 27th May 1918 the 8th Leicestershire Battalion was to the right flank of Chemin des Dames, and lay in the angle formed by the River Aisne and the Aisne Canal.

The morning opened with a thunderous German barrage and their communication was badly disrupted by severed telephone wires. Some forward positions were totally annihilated, and when the enemy infantry worked a pincer movement along the canal they were able to cut off and force units of the Battalion to surrender. Walter Handford was among those brave men who had no option but to lay down their arms.

'Pop had a terrible imprisonment. He was taken all the way through France, Belgium and Germany to an island off Stralsund on the Baltic coast.

In places cattle trucks were used to transport them, and other times they marched through German villages where it was clear they were despised. I try to think what it must have been like for my dear Pop. He was just a quiet churchman, and climbing down from being on Cloud Nine after his recent marriage.

His faith in God carried him through, and he never lost it. The island was in such an isolated spot, that the Red Cross were slow in feeding information back regarding prisoners of war.

Mother was living at 95, Highfield Street, Coalville, when she received a telegram from the War Office briefly stating her husband was: 'Missing believed killed in action'. She was distraught; they had only been married about eight weeks.

Pop said that a fellow prisoner tried to escape in a barrel, but he was never seen or heard of again. Mother's grief was only tempered when Reverend Hoskins received a list of possible prisoners with Walter's name on, but it had to be confirmed by the War Office. Eventually it was and mother immediately started sending Red Cross parcels.

After the war in January 1919, when father returned home he said some of the parcels reached him, but they were always cut-open, searched for weapons and there was always pilfering.

He survived a terrible six months and returned to Louth, Lincolnshire and finally home. Mother said he was a terrible but wonderful sight, skin and bone and lousy with fleas.'

Earlier, the Coalville Times of the 20th November 1918 reported that Lieutenant Walter Handford had sent a letter to his wife. Its contents explained that he was captured at the same time as Captain Frederic Scott, and that the latter had been killed after being taken prisoner.

The same newspaper on the 10th January 1919 announced the welcome return of Walter after his German imprisonment. It also stated that Mr. W. V. Scott, stationmaster of Coalville's N.W. Railway Station had received a letter from another soldier, who witnessed the burial of his son whilst under German guard, after he'd been shot. The brave Captain was the town's first soldier to receive the Military Cross, and his younger brother, Clifford, had been one of the Famous Fifty and had been killed at Ypres in 1915. Mr. W.V. Scott had believed that Frederic (no k) had been shot through the head in battle, and the article continued that he had forwarded the later reports to the War Office. On the 7th February 1919 his name had not appeared on any casualty list. No more was heard or said until his name suddenly appeared on the Casualty List as the date of capture, 27th May 1918.

The home front in England had changed dramatically over the four war years, and generally speaking, only essential funds were available. Teaching of music was not looked upon as an essential, and it was a source of sadness for Walter to think that several of his brightest pupils had perished during the war.

Joyce continues, 'It was not something he ever enjoyed as a livelihood but he opened a greengrocer shop at 121, Belvoir Road, Coalville. The years passed and Pop devoted a large part of his life to the church. For many years he played the organ at St. Deny's Church at Ibstock, and I was bridesmaid there three times. He then returned to a similar position at St John The Baptist at Hugglescote.

During World War 2, I can remember mother and I visiting local houses to collect the 'Red Cross Penny a Week'. The money was used by the W.R.V.S. (Women's Royal Voluntary Service) for amongst other things, buying and sending food parcels for our prisoners of war. Mother never forgot what Pop had to endure during the earlier conflict. In 1953 I was in Paris with a party of civil servants on an exchange visit with the French P.T.T. We were taken to lots of places including Rheims and surrounding areas. I had my photograph taken and on it a sign to Chateau Thierry was visible. When I showed it to Pop he instantly said that was where he was captured thirty-five years earlier.

When my parents retired they moved to 66, Broom Leys Road, and at the age of seventy-five he ceased playing the organ, his magnificent musical piece. They joined the congregation at St David's Church, Broom Leys where Jabez was a member, and who lived close by. Mother died in 1972 and Pop died from heart failure on the 22nd November 1977 at nearby Markfield Sanatorium. (Walter's ashes are buried in a casket in St. David's Garden of Remembrance). That was the last time I saw Jabez Emmerson, he died a few years later. I was a great friend of his daughter, Jean, until we left school and took

Walter Handford, organist, St John The Baptist Church, Hugglescote.

up our different careers.

Often I would pass through Sawbridgeworth where the 5th Leicestershire Battalion trained. Pop would point out this cottage in Station Road where he was billeted with Jabez, William and Cyril (I think his name was Walton or Crane). We always stopped for two minutes silence, dedicated to the memory of all his pals who died on the battlefields of Europe.

Pop, always modest, he never pushed his abilities or knowledge and he never complained. He was wounded twice in France and never fully recovered from the nightmare of trench life. He will always be my hero.'

Walter was a quiet and reserved man possessing many gentle qualities; he was indeed a gentleman in the very finest sense. I know for a fact that he was very well liked, respected and admired.

Many thanks to Joyce, and also to Walter's nephew, Geoffrey Handford, an old friend.

Isaac Harper

Isaac was born in the 1890s in the village of Hugglescote. Little is known of him, however he worshipped at St. John The Baptist Church and attended the Church School.

Isaac volunteered at Coalville in mid-August into the 5th Leicestershire Battalion and has the service number of 2522. The Coalville Times of the 19th March 1915 has his name listed along with nearly seventy others in a Roll of Honour of 'old boys' now serving in the King's Forces. His serial number and

Battalion is clearly listed with many others in the same battalion. John Harper (below) has the service number of 2523 in the same battalion, but lack of information prevents me from drawing any conclusion other than the obvious. I believe they were brothers or cousins who joined the Colours within minutes of each other. It may have some bearing that an Edward William Harper of 'The Castle Hotel' was a lieutenant in the North Midland M.T.D. Brigade A.S.C.

Isaac Harper survived the war.

John W. Harper

'Jack' was born in 1892 at Hugglescote. His father, also bearing the Christian name, John, was a foreman at Messrs Burgess and Sons, elastic web manufactures of Belvoir Road, and the family lived at 179, Belvoir Road, Coalville. Jack was educated at the Wesleyan School on the same road, and later was employed as a blacksmith's striker by Stableford's Wagon Works. He

enlisted at his hometown during mid-August 1914 into the 5th Leicestershire Battalion. He rapidly won the admiration and respect of his comrades and proved himself a good leader on the field of battle. At the time of his death he was a sergeant in charge of the Lewis-Gun section, under the command of Captain Aubrey Moore of 'C' Company. The Battalion had recently moved to the frontline near to Fosse 3, (Lens Sector) when a shell burst at the entrance of the Company's Headquarters. He was one of seven wounded but died the following day, the 7th June 1917. He was aged twenty-five years. Jack was a single man and had only just returned to the trenches after a spell of home-leave.

Captain Aubrey Moore wrote to his parents:

'It is with deep regret that I have to inform you that your son, Sergeant John Harper has died of wounds received on the night of June 6th. An enemy shell dropped on the road killing and wounding some men who were with your son. Please accept the deepest sympathy of the officers, N. C. O.'s and men of the Company. Your son was a general favourite with everyone and we deplore his loss bitterly. As you no doubt know he was in charge of the Company's Lewis guns, and was a thoroughly capable instructor, and a most valuable man. I shall have a very hard task to replace such a man. He did his duty and was a thorough sportsman, always bright and cheerful. Words fail to express my deep regret in your sad loss. If ever a man did his duty for his country it was your son and he died a soldier.'

Frederick Williamson, another of the Fifty who had

Captain Aubrey Moore

lost his brother in 1916, also wrote to his parents:

'Jack was like a brother to me, a hero and game to the last. He was a soldier through and through and well liked and respected by all the battalion. I saw dear old Jack before he went-up and he was telling me what a good time he had whilst on leave. That was the last I saw of him. The next thing I heard was that he had been badly wounded and died a few hours afterwards. He was like so many others, he gave his life for his friends and you can guess how I felt it. I felt it more because I recently lost my own dear brother. I cannot write much more as I know you will be upset, but in closing let me write that may we be ready when we meet Jack in the land where there is no war. Let us put our trust in the One that sees all.'

Sergeant 'Jack' Harper is remembered on the Coalville Clock Tower Memorial and on a tablet in St. John The Baptist Church at Hugglescote.

Jack's brother, Harold was a lance corporal in the 2/1 Suffolk Yeomanry. (H/305298).

It may be coincidence but an Ernest Harper (40045) M.M. of Belvoir Road died whilst serving with the 7th Leicestershire Battalion on the 10th October 1917. He was twenty years of age and he too worked for Messrs Burgess and Sons. Ernest is remembered on the Coalville Clock Tower Memorial and on a tablet in St. John The Baptist Church at Hugglecote. The article reporting the death of Jack stated his parents had two other sons in the army.

Frederick Wilfred Hart

Frederick was born in 1895 at Burton on Trent in Staffordshire to Mr & Mrs G. C. Hart. Whilst he was a youngster the family moved to 35, London Road at Coalville where his father was assistant-superintendent for an Insurance Company.

He was always amused that by whatever his Christian name, it could be shortened to Fred.

Frederick was a former scholar at the Wesleyan School on Belvoir Road, where his school friends included the Bradshaw brothers and Jack Harper. As a boy he adored the outdoor life and soon joined the Coalville Scout Troop, spending many a week at their

summer camps. His sister, Elsie Ramsell (who died in 2001) told me so much about the big brother she adored: *'He used to play the drums when the scouts held a parade along the London Road, he loved it and we were so proud of him. Fred was a grand lad, full of fun, I couldn't have had a better brother. He used to tell me about sitting around campfires at night-time, and looking at the stars and how food tasted so much better cooked over an open fire in a wood. Several times just before the war he used to camp with a couple of friends close to Forest Rock public house. I used to walk-up Meadow Lane on my own and spend a few hours with him. He was with pals*

Frederick Hart, taken in December 1914 at Sawbridgeworth.

Frederick Hart and Allen Ford, summer 1913 near to Forest Rock, Charnwood Forest. *'I'll clean the teapot if you'll peel the spuds.'*

like Allen Ford, Johnny Lowe and Charlie Jewsbury. As soon as he saw me he would put the kettle on the stove and later we would have a bite to eat. It was lovely up there.'

The L. and N.W.R. Railway at Coalville employed Frederick as a locomotive engine cleaner. An extremely sociable young man who whistled and laughed his way through life, never a care, never a bad thought, he was a caring and helpful friend to just about everyone in town. Frederick (2535) and Charlie Hatter (2534) enlisted together at Coalville in mid-August into the 5th Leicestershire Battalion. Afterwards the pair went for a drink to celebrate receiving the 'King's shilling' and to toast a future victory.

Elsie Ramsell continues, *'I remember the First Fifty camping in a field near to the Forest Rock, opposite to where a school was built. It was a chilly day in autumn when the First Fifty marched up Belvoir Road and a band was playing and the drums were going. There were ever such a lot of people about cheering them on. I never felt so excited and proud, but when I was standing on the platform and watched our Fred get on the train I became really upset. I cried my eyes out. They looked ever so smart in their new uniforms, we were so proud of them all. We kept on waving until the train disappeared round the bend, and they did the same to us. Our Frederick sent us several letters and a postcard from France.'*

Letter from Sawbridgeworth (dated 25th February 1914).

'My dear sister Maggie,

Just a line in haste to let you know that we leave Sawbridgeworth at 11.30 pm tonight. I received your letter an hour ago for which I thank you very much for it has bucked me up. It is fine to think that I am not forgotten. By the time you get this there is no telling where we shall be, but you can depend on me letting you have a letter as soon as I get to write again. I have had a letter from dad, it is quite mild but different from what I expected. Must close now as we have a lot to do and little time to do it. Thank you for your kind wishes. Can you spot me on the photograph?

Your loving brother, Fred.'

Reading between the lines it appears as though his parents, especially his father, objected to him enlisting. A period of excitement and uncertainty develops within the battalions prior to embarkation, and

Fred Hart and Johnny Lowe at camp. Spring Hill, Charnwood Forest. Spring 1914.

Frederick was looking for, and received, a few warm sentiments to 'buck him up'.

Postcard from France (Dated the 26th May 1915)

'My dear sister Maggie,

Just a card as we have not much time to write. What a day - we have spent so much time digging. Received your parcel and thank you very much for the cake, we have just finished it for tea and we found it delicious. It is a very hot day today, simply the ideal weather for a getaway.

Your ever-loving brother, Fred.'

On the 8th June 1915, the Battalion was on the slopes of Spanbroekmolen (Hill 76) in the Messines Sector of Belgium. Whilst preparing for 'lookout duty' Frederick had been having a chat in the trenches to Private Charles Hatter. He repeated how much he missed Charlie Jewsbury, his pal from scouting days. Fred said that Charlie was killed instantly when he and two others were washing in an old shell-hole when a barrage came over. One shell exploded nearby and the other two suffered shell shock but survived. Frederick couldn't believe he had only spoken to Charlie just twenty minutes before he died.

In the personal effects sent back to Mr and Mrs Jewsbury was an unfinished letter: *'Simply glorious day. Day five in the trenches soon to leave for a rest. Quiet during the day more fun at nights.'* Several lads had already been sniped in the shallow trenches and they were being deepened when Frederick returned to his lookout role. Frederick's suspicion had been aroused and he had just told one of his pals to keep down, when a rifle shot was heard and a bullet entered his chest. A friend described the scene, *'He sank to his knees with a look of puzzlement, stunned. He then fell over backwards trapping his knees under his body. We pulled him in but we knew he was dead the bullet had passed through his heart, and he'd lost a lot of blood.'*

Johnny Lowe sent a letter from France to Mr and Mrs G. C. Hart, writing:

'I feel very much for the two of them, Fred and Charlie, as they were the best all-round fellows that I have ever spoken to. We buried Fred the day he died and I will continue to look after it while I'm in the locality.'

Johnny was one of the Fifty. Private Albert William Hanson wrote that: *'Fred was popular with the lads and will be greatly missed.'*

Private Alan Evans of Ashby de la Zouch wrote: *'He was cheerful and trustworthy.'*

Frederick was just 20 years of age when he met his death, and has slept for many a year now. His scouting companions and soldier pals are still by his side under a starry canvas.

Frederick's name can be read on the Coalville Clock Tower Memorial and on a tablet in the Wesleyan Church.

Many thanks to a kind old lady, the now deceased Elsie Ramsell, sister to Frederick. Elsie asked me to always refer to her brother by his full name, and I am only too pleased to have done so.

Charles Hatter

Charlie, my dear grandfather was born at Hugglescote on the 26th April 1894 to Mr & Mrs C. Hatter. One of four sons with Tom, Harry and Joe and four sisters, Sarah, Hetty, Mary and Nellie, however, Mary died when she was only a little girl.

He enjoyed a happy family life right up to the Great War at 13, Forest Road in the village.

Charles senior was born at Thringstone in 1862 and left school at the age of eight. He had a high percentage of Irish blood flowing through his veins and was an extremely tall man for his century, standing well over six feet in height and powerfully built. A skilled blacksmith, renowned for the high quality of his workmanship, he was persuaded to continue working at South Leicestershire Colliery until his eightieth year. Undoubtedly a tough character and no-man's fool, a firm believer in fair play and justice, but possessing a kindly nature and his heart was in the right place. Mary, his wife was a slight woman of just over five feet tall who was in service at Bardon Hall until her marriage. Mary was loving, mildly natured, caring and generous, always maintaining a very clean and tidy household. Young Charlie worshipped at St John The Baptist Church, and was also a pupil at the Church

The Hatter brothers. Top left: Harry, top right: Charlie, bottom left: Joe, bottom right: Tom.

Hetty played the chapel organ, and the Palmer family were devout Baptists and life-long friends of the Baker family.

Charles Hatter, standing third from right, aged 6.

School, which can be seen on the corner of Station Road and Grange Road. At school were many relatives including his cousin, Bernard Hatter and good friends William (Bill) Massey, Bill Cowley, Cecil Beadman, Jack Harper and the cousin of his future wife, Arthur Newberry Choyce. Charlie was always popular and respected at school; taking after his mother and generally was of an easy-going disposition, and caring and protective towards those in need. He had a Saturday job, delivering bread from a bakery that is still on Forest Road. Although bright, family needs came first, and as a youngster undertook a blacksmith-apprenticeship at Stableford's Wagon Works. He furthered his education at night school, also spending time at college, but it is unsure what subject(s) he studied, although politics was a possibility.

Bill Massey and Charlie were best friends and they took-up amateur boxing around 1910, becoming extremely adroit at the sport and displayed their skills to many an audience on the county circuit.

During the summer of 1914 the engagement was announced of Charlie to Hetty Palmer of 168, Central Road (then known as 43, North Street) in the same village. Her father, John Henry Palmer, had died when he was only 28 years of age from Bright's disease of the kidneys. Her mother, Esther, held the responsibility to bring-up Hetty, sister Florrie and brother, Jack, alone. During the couple's courtship they regularly worshiped at Ebenezer Chapel on the Ashby Road of Coalville.

When the smouldering of discontent erupted into the volcanic heat of war on the 4th August 1914, hastily printed war posters urged volunteers to enlist. The local 5th Leicestershire Battalion urgently required fifty men to top-up the battalion strength, and it was Bill Massey who took the lead and suggested they sign on the dotted line, which they did in mid August. Charlie's brother, Harry was a member of the Church Lads' Brigade and Baden Powell's Scout Movement. He was very keen to enlist and in early August 1914 was desperately dejected when informed that he had a 'weak heart' being declared unsuitable for military service. I understand he suffered with rheumatic fever as a child, and this may have weakened a heart-valve, but it rarely caused a problem and my strongly built relative survived into his eighties. I liked great uncle Harry, a brilliant ballroom dancer and a man of considerable charm, but was never slow in pointing out social injustice when he saw it. Also, because he focussed closely on his brother's military service he was able to impart considerable knowledge to me after my grandfather's death. The other two brothers, Tom and Joe were colliers, and also colourful characters in their own right.

Charles Hatter the blacksmith. Back row, second from right, circa 1912.

During my teenage years grandfather, Private Charles Hatter (2534), refused to discuss the 1914-18 War. He would simply look down and solemnly and slowly shake his head. Later, as a student and well read, I explained my comprehension of the subject and urged him to share his military experiences. Additionally in 1964 (the 50th Anniversary), there was a magnificent series on B.B.C. Television covering the Great War, and lots of newspaper coverage.

I loved my grandfather dearly, and felt that it was important to share his memories. I believed it was necessary for my generation to come to terms with how two World Wars had scarred our society. Gradually the following experiences were scribbled down fifty years after the conflict. The knowledge and awareness imparted to me enhanced my love and respect for him (if that could be so). Also it focussed my respect, compassion and understanding for all who have endured military conflict or suffering in general. Grandfather was quietly spoken, caring and of philanthropic nature. Witnessing the suffering of his fellow man during four horrific years of warfare mentally scarred him, and this strengthened the latter two aspects of his character. When supporting humanitarian values he would speak powerfully, fervently and positively, and this came across particularly in Trades Union matters.

He touched upon his war years a little at a time over several months. Even though we were alone in his cottage, (Hetty was hospitalised for years prior to her death in 1966) he often spoke in a whisper. There was the excitement of the early months after enlistment, and the brotherly spirit within the Fifty. (Following

marriage my grandparents moved into 55, North Street, next door to where the Cowley family once lived. One of the Fifty, Bill Cowley was born there, and it was later re-addressed: 182 Central Road, Hugglescote).

They were proud of their new uniforms, although some required serious adjustments prior to their departure. Charlie, in spite of possessing a strong constitution found early training quite gruelling, and this was typically the case. Generally speaking these early volunteers were rural and small-town lads, hard working, fit and strong, and in a complimentary vein not in the least 'street wise.' Although relatively poor in terms of wealth, they ate homegrown food and had plenty of fresh air and exercise. They were a hardy bunch, and this was just as well. A feature that senior officers noted was their superior night vision over 'city lads' whilst on evening manoeuvres.

At Luton grandfather explained how he unwillingly used his boxing skills a few times. One or two of the Fifty were subject to bullying from within the main Battalion. He firmly believed in assisting the underdog, never prepared to watch others being bullied. Charlie had to intervene, and at the bully's insistence a fight, usually discreet (behind a cowshed) always ended with a black eye for the opponent and an amicable shaking of hands. Bill Massey followed suit on a few occasions, but after early problems the Battalion was of good spirit and morale.

Grandfather spoke of the rough crossing over the Channel. I can see him sitting by the black fire-range in his cottage; wearing a flat cap on his head to keep the afternoon sun from his eyes, and shaking his head as he told me of one of the Battalion's first deaths: *'My old pal, Sam Boot. After all of that training and I don't think he ever fired his gun in anger. He was sniped through the head, killed outright when he was on sentry duty.'* On the evening of April 15th 1915 at Spanbroekmolen, Hill 76 on the Messines Ridge. The same applied to all the early deaths, such as Fred Hart. *'We enlisted into the Tigers at the same time and enjoyed a quick drink, we were all good pals. He was in our Company and a sniper shot him in the chest.'*

At the Sunday School Anniversary service held on 23rd April 1915, at a packed Ebenezer Chapel the Pastor read out the names of thirty-nine men who were

Charles Hatter, standing on the right, 6th June 1917, a day before the battle of Fosse 3. Lens.

Isaac Hall and Walter Gray were killed by the blast. Lots of others died, their bodies never found.

Grandfather told me of one of the lads who enlisted just before him in mid-August 1914. *'He always had a confident air about him, it was no surprise to hear of his bravery. He was a pal by the name of Corporal (later Captain) Jabez Emmerson.'*

Charlie's first wound came four days after Bill Massey had sent a postcard home, reassuring everyone that all was fine, and mentioning: 'Charlie is all right.' After a break from the frontlines the 5th Battalion was bivouacked at Maple Copse, close to Sanctuary Wood, when the enemy artillery shelled the area. There were only a few dugouts and most took cover behind tree trunks. Thirty-five men were either killed or wounded. Pte Charles Hatter was stunned and peppered by shrapnel following a shell exploding near to him, and was sent to hospital for treatment and recuperation. Bill was confident that his pal would recover, and he was correct, however, they were never to meet again. On the 8th August 1915, Bill was sniped through the head whilst on sentry duty. He was buried nearby, but the ground was fought over many times and his remains were never found. His name is remembered on the Menin Gate Memorial. It was a measure of their friendship that Bill's name was often mentioned right up to the death of grandfather.

I was told that when the Battalion was in the Salient, a dreadful rumour passed around about the Germans crucifying a Canadian soldier. Nothing else was heard and after the war it was looked upon as allied propaganda, for it certainly instilled a greater hatred for the 'Hun.'

Only recently has such an event been substantiated. On the 24th April 1915 a Sergeant Harry Band of 'C' Company, 15th Battalion, the 48th Canadian Highlanders, was crucified onto a barn door using bayonets. They were embedded into his wrists, feet and lower abdomen parts. Harry was born in Montrose in 1885 and had recently emigrated to Toronto, but

serving in the Forces. Men in the 5th Leicestershire Battalion mentioned were Fred Briers, Arthur Green, Charles Hatter, Victor Woolley, Frederick Williamson, John Bullock and Walter Gray.

Whilst in Trench 50 near to Hill 60 in the Ypres Salient, Swannington man, William Wardle was sniped in the heart on July 4th. William was a September volunteer and a 2/5th Battalion man, however when a few of the 1/5th men were reposted he joined the Battalion and embarked for France in February 1915. During the same tour grandfather said that one early evening (July 19th), a nearby Division detonated a huge mine under German trenches at Hooge. The blast was terrific and he recalled that for a long time debris fell from the skies around their trench, and some of it was clearly clothed in smouldering German grey.

Charlie was very relieved when on the 23rd July 1915 he rescued Bill Massey after the enemy blew a mine under their trenches. Bill was shaken and partly buried, but his best pal frantically dug him out, and in turn they saved others. *'We were expecting something to happen but it was still a real shock, and so violent. There was screaming and shouting of orders, it was darkish and you could hear the wounded groaning, I just found a shovel and did my best like all the other survivors. I heard Bill shout my name, he was nearby and I dug him out he was all right!'* Three of the First Fifty, George Andrews, decided to immediately return to help fight for the motherland. The Germans had tortured Harry following their frustration at having failed to breakthrough after the (their) first use of gas. The unpardonable incident took place near to St. Julien, only four kilometres north of Sanctuary Wood.

During late September a letter from his parents informed Charlie that his cousin, 2nd Lieutenant Bernard Hatter of North Street, Hugglescote had been killed. Bernard was in the 2nd Leicestershire Battalion and he was mortally wounded. He fell into enemy trenches whilst leading a bayonet charge on the 15th September at the Battle of Loos, France. His body was never found. A few weeks later on October 13th, grandfather went over the top at the Battle of Hohenzollern, only a few kilometres north of the village of Loos.

In terms of violence, bloodshed, and depths of tiredness this was his nightmare for many years: *'On the day before we marched ten miles in 'fighting order' (carrying sixty pounds - twenty-seven kilograms) and arrived at the trenches late at night. We remained in them, like sardines in the trench and didn't sleep and we never had any breakfast or much to drink. In early afternoon we scrambled up the trench ladders and bayonet-charged the enemy redoubt, but dead men from the 4th Battalion were everywhere, and little wonder with the machine-gun fire and shells. Jerry counter-attacked but our Captain Langdale (he always had a pipe in his mouth, even then) waved us on. Our lads were falling all over the place cut to ribbons and we had some hand-to-hand fighting it was bad stuff. I didn't eat until the following day, and I was relieved the next day (15th). During the night we walked back to camp, we were pleased to be out of it, and so we had a bit of a singsong.'*

I possess two or three postcards that he bought whilst on his 'fruitless' trip to Marseilles. He enjoyed this little escape from the trenches, the blue of the Mediterranean and a milder climate, but he said he 'wasn't up' for going to Egypt or the Dardanelles. Grandfather continued: Vimy Ridge. *'The conditions were grim, wet and very cold and a lot of the lads went down with 'trench foot' so painful it made men crawl in agony. The skin rotted and peeled off. Our Captain got killed there and Lieutenant Moore took over. Both very good officers and men. (Captain Roland Farmer and later Captain Aubrey Moore). Another old school friend, Bill Cowley disappeared when mining.'*

The Somme. *'The barrage was ever so loud and the ground shook, especially when Jerry sent some of his big shells onto our trenches. Very wet, the sides of the trenches were caving in and it was just a confusing blur of yelling, swearing and dead bodies lying around.'*

Lens 1917. *'When we attacked we often took shelter in ruined houses and sometimes in cellars. I was alone in this house when I saw some Jerries walking by a window. I hadn't realised our lads had retired and Jerry had advanced, it was like that then. I hid in an old wardrobe and they chatted away and smoked. I knew that if I was found they would kill me. No side took prisoners in the suburbs. When they left I had a careful look around and then scampered back to my mates.'*

June 1917 at Fosse 3. *'It was like a bad dream. Just unreal at night with us black figures fighting in the red glow of fires, savage bayoneting, and the hand-to-hand stuff. Jerry fought hard on that night, we were all fighting for our lives.'*

I have a photograph of Charlie the day before this attack. A few weeks later, a follow-up attack led to many of 'C' Company dying from gas asphyxiation.

July 1917. *'We were back in the Loos area (Hulluch) and the Battalion was involved in a raid on the German lines. It was pitch dark again and I remember getting a thud in the back.*

I couldn't move and just lay there for three nights and two days. One or two other lads were groaning but they stopped a little later, they must have died. I thought it was my end, and had lots of thoughts of home, but I wasn't in great pain and in time believed I would survive. On the third night a tingling-feeling started and I crawled back to our trenches. I was sent to a hospital in France, it might have been near to Reims, and I made a full recovery.'

Only after his death did I discover that he still had a bullet lodged in (or near) his backbone. Grandfather never told me it wasn't removed, apparently the surgeons considered it unwise, especially with original wound causing no problems. At least we are not aware of him complaining as such. His sister, Nellie, told me about his bullet and was later confirmed by his son, my uncle Maurice.

A pendant made from bullets
by Charles Hatter.

The German's Spring Offensive of March 1918. *'We weren't really involved too much, but I had another whiff of gas and I was out of the frontline for a week or two.'* This may have been where Captain Moore and forty-three other ranks were gassed in the La Bassee Sector. (Most of the troops suffered the effects of gas on more than one occasion).

Grandfather always had a bad cough, and when he returned from the war in 1919 he could not take to his earlier job as blacksmith, due to forge-smoke. His brother, Harry, went with him to London to fight for a war pension. The authorities were sympathetic but said they 'could not possibly afford to compensate all the gas casualties'.

Pontruet - 24th September 1918. *' That was where an officer of ours won the Victoria Cross for leading a charge against a machine-gun post. (Forgan's Trench) A brave man, he got badly wounded, we hoped that he wouldn't die and he didn't. A very fit man who swore more than most, it was just his way. He became a surgeon at the Leicester Royal Infirmary after the war. It was a bad day, dark and misty. Other brave men getting killed trying to help others, they received no decorations. It was difficult to see what was happening, warfare was always confusing, and you had to avoid becoming isolated. I remember one lad being hit by machine-gun bullets from his upper legs to his lower abdomen including his private parts. He went berserk and died very quickly.'* I believe grandfather was in 'C' Company, which was closest to Forgan's Trench from an attacking point of view but I cannot verify whether he took part in the charge, which resulted in Lieutenant J.C. Barrett receiving the Victoria Cross.

'After this battle I'd had enough of the war, I was all in and my cough was very bad and so my officer allowed me to do some paper work for him. Also I helped out in the stores.' (Grandfather finished as a frontline soldier after three and a half years and I think it was William Emmerson who kept an eye on him and treated him very well).

The Hindenburg Line. *'It was something of a big victory for the Division, but when I was delivering to the lads all I remember is a long ridge and a lot of dead and dying all around. After we crossed a canal the fighting was very tough going, and I lost more old pals. They sent me home for some leave and I got married on the 4th November 1918 at Ebenezer Baptist Chapel. After the ceremony we went to your Grandma's house, 168, Central Road for a party, and I remember my dad climbing on the table and singing: 'Keep the whole-wide-world-a-turning'. I returned to the Battalion just before the Armistice. We were all pleased to have survived the war, but then it sank in about the pals we'd lost. Early in the New Year I came home for good. It was a bad job.'* (Shaking head).

Around this time (1964-5) he gave me one or two keepsakes from the war. A highly treasured possession is his engagement ring from 1914. Inscribed on the ring are the initials 'CHP', namely 'Charlie Hatter - Hetty Palmer'. This was on my grandfather's finger throughout the entire war (if only gold could speak). My grandmother wore an engagement ring and a locket around her neck, which contained a small photograph of her fiancé, which I also have.

My grandparent's marriage was blessed with a daughter, Betty, born in 1920 and a son, Maurice in 1923. During World War 2 my mother was in the Auxiliary Territorial Service A.T.S. 602 Heavy Ack-Ack Anti-Aircraft Battery. Uncle Maurice, after originally serving in the Leicestershire Regiment, fought in North Africa with the Green Howards until being badly wounded. Mother and uncle married their respective partners in the 'Forties' and continue to have happy lives.

Grandfather, like his father before him was a strong trade unionist, and he served the Transport and General Workers Union for fifty years, being branch secretary for over twenty of them. Mr. Phillip Snowden. M.P. and grandfather were responsible for introducing the Labour Party into Coalville, and naturally this made him friends as well as some enemies.

Phillip Snowden, president of Ellistown Miner's Welfare Committee, was also a notable author for the Socialist Library, and a close compatriot of J. Ramsay MacDonald.

Hetty and Charlie Hatter on their 30th Wedding Anniversary, 4th November 1948.

During the turbulent nineteen-twenties and thirties Charlie was often sacked for defending fellow workers, and this led to hand to mouth living, but he was a determined character with high standards and led by example. Lifelong friend Jabez Emmerson, one of the Fifty tried to persuade him to accept the position of Justice of the Peace in the early Fifties. He politely refused: *'I do not wish to judge my fellow man.'*
My personal opinion is that strong-minded men like grandfather did an awful lot to improve the living conditions of ordinary workingmen, and the status quo continues to this day.

I must have appeared terribly naïve when I asked: *'You are a clever man, a leader, a brave soldier, why is it that you finished four years of warfare as a private?'* He didn't hesitate as he replied: *'I could not accept the responsibility of leading my friends to their deaths.'*

In the early 1960's grandmother had a 'serious stroke' and grandfather took care of her at home for several years. Another haemorrhage meant hospitalisation in Market Bosworth until her death on the 24th February 1966. Grandmother had a very difficult life, but everyone who knew her commented on her caring nature and how she was prepared to help all and sundry.

Her sister, my great-auntie Florrie (Flo) lost her fiancé in the war and never married and the dear lady shared her sister's virtues, and both were devout Baptists. Their brother, Jack Reed Palmer served in the Leicestershire Yeomanry and survived the war. For the remainder of his working life he worked on the coalface. He was a very quiet man, something of a loner and I was told that he was concealing bitter memories from the Great War. Like so many others his youthful mind was scarred and it blighted much of his life.

Bad health plagued grandfather's final years, *'A lonely man, missing a wife of an earlier time.'* I remember an occasion in 1968, he was gravely ill with heart problems, Parkinson's disease and pneumonia. In his delirium he was reliving his war years. It was instantaneous stuff, various horrors as they occurred in his mind. He was at fever pitch and beads of perspiration sat on his brow. I grasped his hand and spoke gently and reassuringly to him. His breathing grew easier and his eyes flickered and finally opened. Unable to smile, Parkinson's disease had paralysed his facial muscles, his face was like a mask but his eyes reflected the dear love I felt for him. I will never forget the visit, and from that moment on I have felt tremendous compassion and understanding for all folk who suffer. After two years at Tillson House, a council retirement home in Coalville, he passed away on the 24th January 1970.

Another memory is of my great-auntie Nellie, grandfather's youngest sister. I was told:

'I watched the First Fifty march pass Baxton's Corner (corner at the junction of Forest Road and Central Road) and followed the procession all the way to the station. I was so proud of Charlie, but I could not stop the tears from flowing. About a year afterwards I was thrilled when my brother came home for a short leave. After a few days I was next door at number 15, Forest Road with a little girl of the Burton family, and we were scraping some cake-mixture from a bowl. Charlie came in, picked me up, kissed me and said: 'I've got to go now.' Nellie continued, *'I just could not stop myself from crying for ages, so many local men were being killed at that time.'* Nellie received beautiful postcards and letters from the front, today treasured by her daughter, Doreen Johnson. (The Burton family had a son, William who was fighting abroad at the time and survived the war).

A further memory comes from his niece, Freda. Although only a young girl and living on Grange Road, Hugglescote - near to the church, she remembers the night a Zeppelin airship passed over their home, over the church and headed towards Ellistown Colliery. *'People were in the street, and I could see this German airship from my bedroom window. It looked ghostly in the sky, a bit frightening and it made me think of my Uncle Charlie in France. He was my favourite uncle, a very kind and gentle man, we all loved him.'* Another niece, Jenny, said Charlie was also her favourite uncle.

Grandfather enjoyed his pint at Coalville's Half Way House or the Labour Club, and was pretty good at darts and dominoes. Always a keen supporter of Leicester City Football Club, he watched many a game at Filbert Street when funds were available, and loved to chat about the County Cricket Club.

I have a vivid memory of one glorious summer's morning when I cycled the eight miles to spend the day with grandfather. Entering through the door he enthusiastically greeted me.

It was clear he was beaming with joy and emotion. The year was 1964 and Harold Wilson had taken the Labour Party into power. *'It's the Party of the working man, given time the poor will have a greater share of the country's wealth.'* Typical Charlie, he was seventy years of age and as poor as a church mouse, but he would not have included himself in his statement.

For most of their married life my grandparents lived at the rented little terraced cottage of 180, Central Road, Hugglescote. I cannot imagine what memories went through Charlie's mind, especially in his lonelier years, as he walked down the cinder path at the rear of the cottages. The picture of the Famous Fifty was taken on Friday 30th October 1914 at the rear of 168, Central Road, his fiancée's home. How often did he see in his mind's eye those bright-eyed young soldiers, many of who were soon to perish in France and Flanders?

William Newbold, another of the Fifty lived at 177, Central Road for several years before the Great War. Young Charlie knew him well; they went to the same Church and Church School.

How often did grandfather glance over the road, and imagine seeing William as a boy or as a young man in khaki? As a man he died of appalling injuries at

Arthur Newberry Choyce.

Polygon Wood at Ypres.

Living next door to William at 177, Central Road was Arthur Newberry Choyce, cousin of Hetty Hatter and famed as Leicestershire's Great War poet. After being wounded at Arras in 1917, the Military authorities sent him to tour the United States of America to recite his war poetry and help with enlistment there. He wrote several books of poetry and also a semi-biographical novel: 'Lips at the Brim', about his upbringing in a mining village and his time in the army and the U.S.A. Arthur died on the 2nd February 1937 at the age of forty-three. At the terraced-cottage next door, 182, Central Road, lived until shortly before the Great War one of his best friends, Bill Cowley, who was entombed by a mine-blast in 1916.

Grandfather was a caring, compassionate, intelligent, generous and gentle man who shied-away from material possessions or social position. He invariably went out on a limb to help others, especially the underprivileged. He died penniless, leaving a wealth of philanthropic standards of which few could attain. My grandparents now lie in eternal peace in Hugglescote's Station Road Cemetery. Their headstone is relatively new and etched upon it is a Flanders Poppy. 'Until we all meet again'. Shortly after his death I wrote the following poem.

I have purposely expressed my inner feelings, and may readers understand that similar emotions apply to all members of the Fifty from their relatives. It cannot be over-emphasised the impact the Great War had upon them and how the reverberations have effected subsequent generations including society to this day. To forget the horrors of the two Twentieth Century Wars would be the equivalent of mankind stumbling forward whilst wearing a death mask.

GRANDFATHER

The evening chill crept into my skin,
As the dusky light relaxed the tension within my eyes.
Street lamps blinked into life to create the colour of sunset,
And so support the moon as bearer of light.
My footsteps echoed on the cobbled pathway
As I approached grandfather's cottage.

The rocking chair was still, or did it rock?
Perhaps it wanted to, as I wanted it to, but it did not!
Old friends, leather boots were sitting by the fire.
Solid wax tears of polish trickled to the tiled floor,
And to the memory of a companion, survive an eternity of mopping.
Grandfather, I know you, I feel you, but I know not where you are.

Oh, grandfather, how you suffered on Great War battlefields,
How you toiled for others in life now is the time to rest.
Your silvery white hair, it was you,
A white flag of goodness and maturity.
Those eyes, those large healing orbs
That soothed many a cut and bruise on a little body.

A cap was finely balanced on a nail in the wall,
And on the table, lay uncomfortably a wrinkled cloth.
A solitary and forlorn shirt hung grimly to a door handle,
And the chime on the old wall-clock had stopped for all time.
Sorrow, the cottage had the touch of a single man,
A lonely man, missing a wife of an earlier time.

On the bare, cracked walls hung black and white photographs,
Framed reminders of what was and how things came to be.
A pictorial life tree, with each photograph being but a branch,
And each branch is of likeness.
The living seeds of grandfather in his children and children's children.
Grandfather, I know you, I feel you, and I know where you are!

For the memories of grandfathers everywhere, especially for my own, Charles Hatter 1894-1970.
(Written in the summer of 1970)

Arthur William Hodgetts

Always known as Dennis, he was born at Leicester on the 16th May 1897. His father, also named Arthur (hence the name Dennis) was a riveter, working in the lasting department of a local boot and shoe factory. His mother's name was Florence. Following a slump in footwear manufacture Arthur moved the family to 234, Ashby Road, Coalville after he obtained employment down the mines.

Arthur (Dennis) and Ethel Hodgetts, early 1920's. Ethel was born in 1899.

Dennis, a very good young footballer, left school and followed his father working at a local colliery. Life was looking rosy until the outbreak of the Great War. He enlisted at Coalville in mid-August into the 5th Leicestershire Battalion. During the next three years, Dennis experienced some appalling situations and great emotional upheavals. He faced heavy shell bombardments, machine-gun fire, asphyxiating gas, trench mortars, and sniping. We must not forget he would regularly have been forced to wade knee deep in polluted, smelly water, be bitten by meat eating rats, riddled with fleas, suffered thirst, hunger and extremes of temperature, whether by day or night. He went 'over the top' in such battles as Ypres, Hohenzollern (Loos), Vimy Ridge and the Somme. At some time during the final year he was wounded or possibly gassed, and did not recover until after the Armistice.

Shortly after the war Dennis left the pits and decided to train as an electrician with Balfour and Beatty, and he successfully did so. Life and health continued to improve and on the 21st December 1921 he married Hugglescote girl, Ethel Mary Hoden at

The Hodgetts family, early 1920's. Back row: Annie, Ethel, Dennis, Maurice Toon and Ada. Front row: Cecil, Aunt Ada, father, Arthur, mother, Florence and Lillian.

Christ Church, Coalville. The scene was of great happiness and joy and several ex-army friends were present for the occasion. The couple spent several happy years residing at nearby 205, Ashby Road, Coalville. Their first born, Dorothy, was the icing on their cake and sealed a marriage of deep love and contentment. Bliss however was swiftly followed by despair when in quick succession two sons were stillborn. On the 2nd March 1932 Ethel gave birth to a second daughter, Jean. Utter sadness then confronted the family circle. Three days after the birth Ethel died from complications on March 5th. Dennis was absolutely distraught. His parents immediately came to help with Dennis, his young daughter and babe-in-arms moving into 234, Ashby Road. His parents already had three girls and two boys of their own living there. (Daughter Jean can't say enough about the goodness and kindness of her grandparents). Dennis, forever strong and brave battled on the best he could, and enjoyed his lighter moments when his excellent footballing skills enabled him to play for Coalville Town F.C.

Coalville Town F.C. 'Dennis' is on the left of the front row.

Arthur (Dennis) holding Jean outside 234, Ashby Road, Coalville.

Tragedy seems to follow some families like a predator, and in 1938 Dennis was to die in the most severe and cruellest of circumstances. As a highly experienced electrician he was correcting a fault on some electrical wiring, and was strapped to the top of a supporting pole. The power had been safely turned-off at source, but a person committed a dreadful error by pulling the lever, which resulted in Dennis receiving the full electrical force through his body. The veteran of the Great War died instantaneously. The incident happened near to the corner of Market Street at Coalville.

Life seemed always to be unkind to that young family, but future happiness came when Jean married John Huddlestone, and further delight followed with the birth of two children, Linda and Martin. The following generation has also presented two grandchildren, Connor and Robyn.

Certainly Dennis had a few years of happiness, but it is difficult to comprehend the veil of misfortune, grief and sadness that some families have to contend with. Dennis witnessed a mixed-measure of life and was just over forty years of age when he died. Please ensure that his suffering, hardship and selflessness of effort are never forgotten.

Many thanks to Dennis's daughter, Jean and to her husband, John Huddlestone.

Cecil Hurley. D.C.M.

Cecil was born in 1896. He resided with his parents at 'Fernleigh Cottage', Donisthorpe, a village five kilometres (three miles) southwest of Ashby de la Zouch. He enlisted at Ashby in late August 1914. Little is known of the man's early life, but he must have been a collier for he volunteered for Lieutenant Aubrey Moore's counter-tunnelling section in the spring of 1915. Cecil was in good company, working alongside him were men of the calibre of Jabez and William Emmerson, Bill Cowley, Bill Toon, Harry Starbuck and William Barney. Clearly, he was a very brave man for undertaking this highly dangerous activity, and for his courageous displays was awarded the Distinguished Conduct Medal. (D.C.M.).

To confirm the high-esteem by which I hold the colliers of northwest Leicestershire, I refer to an article in the Coalville Times of the 22nd October 1915. '*An enthusiastic send-off was given to about fifty Leicestershire miners, who left by the 11.43 am train from Coalville Station on Wednesday morning, on route for France where they will be engaged in special mining work. The men have responded to an appeal recently made for thirty skilled miners from Leicestershire. A large crowd cheered them as the train moved out of the station and the men were in the best of spirits, some of them singing, some playing mouth organs. To the customary question, 'Are we downhearted?' They responded with several roars of 'No' from the sturdy-looking miners as they stood upon the platform prior to their departure.'*

The above miners wouldn't have joined the Leicestershire Regiment; at this stage of the war Tunnelling Companies were being set-up under the auspices of the Royal Engineers.

From 1916 onwards Cecil reverted to the role of an infantryman, and sadly Corporal Cecil Hurley (2579-240255) D.C.M. was killed on active service in the battle of Pontruet on the 24th September 1918. He rests at Bellingcourt British Cemetery, close to his friend George Underwood. It was during this battle that Lieutenant J.C.Barrett was awarded the Victoria Cross. He survived to within seven weeks of the Armistice after risking his life on the Western Front for nearly four years. Such thoughts always remind me of the magnificent poem written by Lieutenant Wilfred Owen M.C. 'Dulce et decorum est pro patria mori.' The old lie!

John Lowe

Always known as 'Johnny'. He was born in 1893 at Coalville to Mr & Mrs Edward Lowe, and the family lived at 35 Oxford Street in the town. Edward was an engine driver at Whitwick Colliery and upon leaving school John found employment at South Leicestershire Colliery. Johnny was a good pal to Frederick Hart and Charlie Jewsbury, and in addition they were in the same Coalville Scout Troop. Often the three, together with another of the team, Allen Ford, would pack-up and spend a weekend camping in the dappled shade at nearby Charnwood Forest. Frederick Hart's sister, Elsie Ramsell mentioned more than once how excited they became before camping: *'They loved the fresh air and outdoor life, and in the evening twilight sat around a woody fire to brew tea and chat away.'* To all of the First Fifty the 1912-14 period was looked upon as a special time, and with the aforementioned four it was the best times of their lives!

Charlie enlisted at Coalville in February 1914 into the 5th Leicestershire Battalion, 'A' Company, and was trained as a gunner.

Johnny enlisted at Coalville in mid-August 1914 in the 5th Leicestershire Battalion, around the same time as Frederick. He trained as a gunner and joined Charlie as part of the Machine-gun Corps, under the command of Whitwick's Lieutenant A.T. Sharpe. Neither officers nor men enjoyed the prospect of a machine-gun nest being situated close to them in the trench.

The weapon was so devastating when in use, especially to troops caught in open ground, that as a preliminary to any attack the machine gun posts were always targeted for heavy shelling.

Johnny survived the war in a manner of speaking. Elsie Ramsell informed me that a shell-blast permanently upset the balance of his mind. *'Before the war he was a typical young man but afterwards he had the shakes, it was upsetting to see.'* His brother, Ernest served in the same battalion and survived the war.

William Massey

William Massey, 1914.

Always Bill. He was born in 1895 at Hanley, which is now a suburb of Stoke-on-Trent in Staffordshire. The family moved to 33, Main Street, Hugglescote at the turn of the century, and worshipped at St. John The Baptist Church, with Bill also attending the Church School. He was one of eight children, three of them being girls.

His father, Mr R. Massey owned 'Botanic Brewery' on Forest Road, Hugglescote and they bottled mineral waters, later moving their business to Castle Street at Whitwick. Bill enlisted at Coalville in the first week of the war into the 5th

The Massey family circa 1913. William is on the back row, second right.

Leicestershire Battalion. After doing so he had a chat and persuaded his best pal, Charles Hatter, and he followed soon afterwards.

I wrote earlier that Bill and Charlie were very good boxers, indeed my grandfather often referred with irony that the only person to put him 'on the canvas' was his best friend.

The 'likely lads' were good soldiers and adapted smoothly to the rigours of army life and were very popular. This was especially so at Luton when one or two pre-war soldiers tried 'with unnecessary force' to bully some of the First Fifty. The bond within the Fifty was always very close and for the survivors continued for life.

On the evening of the 23rd July 1915, Bill (2512) was badly shocked and almost totally buried when the enemy detonated a mine under their trench (50) near to Hill 60, Ypres Sector. It is a fact that despite the furore of battle and the smoky twilight, Charlie heard his calls, found him and frantically dug him out. During this event the enemy sent forth a hail of rifle and shellfire. Bill sent the following postcard to his parents. It is dated four days after the explosion-Monday, July 27th 1915.

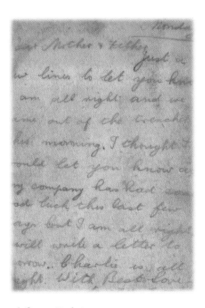

The Postcard from Belgium.
'Dear Mother and Father,

Just a few lines to let you know I am all right, and we came out of the trenches this morning. I thought I would let you know as my company has had some bad luck these last few days, but I am all right. I will write a letter tomorrow. Charlie is all right. With best love to all. Will.'

Only four days after Bill wrote his card Charlie was wounded during a heavy barrage. He was shell-shocked and peppered with shrapnel at Maple Copse near to Zillebeke, Ypres, and forwarded to hospital. The school-chums, the boxers and the soldier-pals - they were never to see each other again.

On the 8th August 1915 Bill was on duty in Trench 50, close to where he was almost buried some two weeks earlier, when he met his death at the age of twenty years.

Private Sidney Summers of 158, Ashburton Road, Hugglescote sent a letter to Bill's parents explaining his grief.

'Monday 9th August 1915.
Dear Mr R.Massey,
Bill was shot through the head when on sentry duty I hope it will be of some consolation to you to know that he died without pain. I was not far off at the time, but did not know it was Bill for some time after. It was about four in the morning. I went to see him when they told me the poor chap had been shot, but they had covered him over so I could not see his face. When they told me it was Bill I could have dropped. He was like a brother to me. We always got on well together and he has been in my thought ever since. I saw him the night before---we had a chat together. He was just as cheerful as ever, and I little thought that would be the last time I would speak to him. Poor old chap.

But we never know whose turn it is, so we can only trust in Him who holds our lives in his hands. He died like a soldier, doing his duty for King and Country. I will find where he is buried and let you know. Break the news quietly to his mother because I know it will be hard to bear. With deepest sympathy to you both at this sad time. Sincerely, Sid Summers.'

Joseph Massey.

Sadly Sid Summers, a Hugglescote man and one of the Fifty died in battle on the 24th September 1918.

Bill was twenty years old when he died. His burial spot was repeatedly fought over during the war years and so no trace of his body survived. His name is remembered on the Menin Gate Memorial, Ypres, Belgium. Also it can be read on the Coalville Clock Tower Memorial and on a tablet in St. John The Baptist Church at Hugglescote.

Bills brother, Joseph also served in the Leicestershire Regiment and survived the war.
Many thanks to Andrew Massey, great nephew of Bill.

William Newbold

William was born in 1896 at Coalville, but as an infant the family moved to 50, North Street (later 175 Central Road, and next door to Arthur Newberry Choyce*) at Hugglescote. The family worshipped at St. John The Baptist Church and William also attended the Church School. He was also a prominent member of Hugglescote's Church Lads' Brigade, and used to sing at the parochial concerts. After leaving school he was employed by the Midland Meat Company of Coalville. If William were still with the Church Lads' Brigade at the outbreak of war he'd have been at the annual camp at Ripon in Yorkshire. He enlisted at Coalville in the first week of the war into the 5th Leicestershire Battalion. William embarked for France in February 1915, but was wounded in the fighting at Ypres in August of the same year. When, after several months he was fully recovered from his wounds he was reposted to Lord Kitchener's New Army, joining the 9th Leicestershire Battalion. It is possible he was involved in the very heavy fighting around the Arras Sector in the early part of 1917 and onwards, and certainly participated in the action at Polygon Wood from 1st October 1917 (Ypres Sector). One of his officers was soldier-poet Lieutenant Arthur Newbury Choyce*. Private William Newbold (2493-40229) was killed in the fighting at the aforementioned Wood on the 31st October 1917.

The Coalville Times of the 30th November 1917, prints a letter sent to his parents from his commanding officer: *'I should like to take the opportunity of saying how highly we all thought of him, and what a really good soldier he was. He was certainly one of the staunchest and most valuable men of my Company, and I offer my deepest sympathy, and that of his comrades.'*

William's name can be read on the Memorial Tablet in St. John The Baptist Church and on the Coalville Clock Tower Memorial.

Walter Pettitt

Walter was born in 1895 at Horm-in-sea in Cambridgeshire to Mr & Mrs Harry Pettitt. Whilst a child the family moved to Hugglescote, and they worshipped at St. John The Baptist Church and Walter attended the Church School there. Just prior to the war the Pettitt family moved yet again to 64, Ibstock Road at Ellistown.

After leaving school Walter obtained employment as a miner at nearby Nailstone Colliery. He enlisted at Coalville in early August 1914 into the 5th Leicestershire Battalion. In the spring of 1915 he volunteered for Lieutenant Aubrey Moore's tunnel counter-mining and was involved in operations at Messines and Ypres. He fought as a frontline soldier at the battle of the Hohenzollern Redoubt and also on the Somme. Walter was awarded one week of home-leave in the latter part of July 1917, and was killed nine days after returning to his unit. After witnessing and suffering the inherent dangers of mining and trench-life Walter was killed in a relatively safe area quite a way from the frontlines. The Battalion had just spent a restful fortnight at Fouquieres in France, when they moved to huts at Noyelles in preparation for a heavy raid against German trenches close to Hulluch, in the St. Elie Left Sector of France.

The purpose of this raid was to detract attention for a Canadian attack that was scheduled on Hill 70, just to the south near Loos. On the 15th August 1917, the day before the raid, the Battalion paraded at 10 am and marched through Vermelles to Lone Trench and Tenth Avenue where they were to await. During the journey 'B' Company was marching in fours past the Mansion House Dump, when an enemy shell fell amongst them. Eleven were killed outright, including Walter (2488-240564) and fourteen others were wounded.

Another soldier who was killed was Freddie Chambers from Easton on the Hill, Lincolnshire, a cheerful man with a sharp wit and a ready supply of jokes. The Coalville Times of the 21st September 1917 reported Walter's death.

Lance Corporal C. Frearson, a Coalville soldier

wrote to his parents:

'Walter was more like a brother to me, and now it seems as if a great cloud has come over, and every joy and pleasure has gone. He died doing his duty like a man, and I hope this will console you. On the battlefield and at sports he was always a giant in himself. Always be merry and bright, was Walter's motto, and many a time he has cheered the whole platoon.'

(Happily the Lance Corporal survived the war).

Lieutenant Chapman wrote that the Company had sustained a great loss by the death of such a magnificent soldier. Walter had been wounded earlier in the war and had three or four narrow escapes. The Coalville

Times stated that on one occasion he was saved by his tin flask that was strapped to his body. Walter took the badly dented flask that was hit by a bullet home, and left it as a keepsake with his parents.

Walter's name appears in the Coalville Times of the 19th of March 1915, in a list submitted by the Church School's headmaster, Mr. F. J. Wainwright. Over sixty names of old-boys in the forces are mentioned. Walters name can be read on St. John The Baptist War Memorial and also at the parish church, Ellistown.

Walter was just 21 years of age when he died, and his name can also be also read on the Coalville Clock Tower Memorial.

Wilfred Robinson

Wilfred was born in 1896 at Hugglescote and lived with his parents at 4, Ashburton Road within the village. The family worshipped at St. John The Baptist and he attended the Church School. Next door lived William Baker, who also attended the school and one of the Fifty. Wilfred (2482) enlisted at Coalville in the first week of the war into the 5th Leicestershire Battalion. He was promoted, the War Diary in August 1917 states: *'Heavy trench-mortars were terrifying and few could face them with indifference, Lance Corporal W.*

Robinson and his Lewis Gun team treated them with scorn, and used rapid rifle fire at them.' Wilfred (53656) was transferred to the 56th Machine-Gun Corps and survived the conflict. Such transfers to this Corps were not uncommon due to the high death rate amongst them, being especially targeted by the enemy artillery. Both houses (number 2 and 4) were demolished in the Thirties and replaced by a detached property built for a schoolmistress.

Thomas Robson

Tom was born in the 1890s and lived on Victoria Street, Ellistown. He held the reputation for being the first man to volunteer from his village into the King's Armed Forces. He enlisted at Coalville in the first week of the war into the 5th Leicestershire Battalion. It was recorded in the Coalville Times of the 11th August 1916 that he had been wounded. Tom's brother, Stewart Robson was killed by shellfire in April 1918 whilst serving with the Machine-Gun Corps. Tom was a good friend of Cliff Scott (whose details follow), for he and Hugglescote's Archie Tovell buried the young son of the Coalville East Stationmaster. Tom (2502) survived the war.

Archie G. Tovell was born in 1894 at 123, North Street (later Central Road) and prior to the war was employed at Burgess's factory on Belvoir Road at Coalville.

He was transferred from the 5th Battalion to the Machine-Gun Corps and lost his life on the 1st February 1917. His brother, Frederick John (222962) was also a gunner in the 466th R.F.A., 65th Brigade. Archie's name can be read on Coalville's Clock Tower Memorial and on a Memorial Tablet in St. John The Baptist Church.

Clifford Ernest Scott

Cliff was born in 1895 at Blaby, once a large village about 5 kilometres (3 miles) south of Leicester City centre and about 25 kilometres (15 miles southeast of Coalville). His father was Station Master there and shortly after Cliff's birth he secured the same position at Coalville East Railway Station. When I study this family history and look at the photographs, I see once again a family blessed with such good fortune and vitality, and yet blighted by the tragedy of war.

Cliff was the last born of four sons, and his mother Kate (nee Smith, 1866-95) tragically died the year he was born. The other three sons were Walter V. Scott (1887-1962), Leonard (Len) George Scott (1889-1946) and Frederic (Fred with no 'k') Scott (1893-1918).

Clifford Scott, telegram messenger.

The father was in the fraught situation of struggling to maintain a full-time job and look after four young sons. After a while he fortunately remarried, to Elizabeth (nee Franklin). They had two further sons, Robert Scott and William Franklin Scott.

Walter, a very dependable man with outstanding caring qualities was also the Superintendent of Coalville's St. John's Ambulance Brigade.

From early years the two youngest sons, Cliff and

Fred were partial to outdoor life; indeed they were keen members of the Y.M.C.A. (Young Men's Christian Association) and spent many a weekend living beneath the starry heavens under canvas.

Upon leaving Coalville Grammar School Cliff became a Telegram Messenger, looking particularly smart in his uniform, and later he obtained a position as a Clerk with the L. and N.W.R. in his hometown.

Cliff enlisted at Coalville in the first week of the war into the 5th Leicestershire Battalion, no doubt encouraged by his elder brother, Frederic.

Clifford Scott, front row first right and his brother Frederic Scott second row, first right.

Frederic was educated at Ashby de la Zouch Grammar School, and would have known Jabez and William Emmerson, Aubrey Moore and Walter Handford. Subsequently, he had a spell as a pupil-teacher at the Coalville's Bridge Road School. He continued with his education at Cambridge University, and joined the University's Officer Training Corps at Mychett in July 1914. He eventually served as a Captain in the 6th Battalion of the Leicestershire Regiment, being wounded at least twice, and was awarded the Military Cross. The Captain died in 1918 at the hands of the Germans whilst a prisoner of war. (See Walter Handford details).

The second eldest brother, Len, also fought in the Great War and survived, later emigrating to the United States of America.

The 5th Battalion's own twenty-year-old Private Cliff Scott (2488) of 'A' Company met his death in the Ypres Sector of Belgium. The location was once again in Trench 50 where so many of 'the pals' died. On the 1st September 1915 our artillery bombarded the

Frederic Scott recovering from injury.

German lines and the Germans retaliated. Initially they sent over salvoes of whizz-bangs, and finished-off with heavy shoot, 8 inch, 5.9s and shrapnel shells. The attack lasted from 10.45 am until mid-day. The War Diary reads: *'In 'A' Company, except for C.S.M. Gorse's and the Signaller's, every dugout was hit, and Privates C. E. Scott and F. W. Pringle, the two officers' batmen were killed, while A. H. Cassell was badly wounded.*

2nd Lieutenant J. Wyndham Tomson had a miraculous escape when a 5.9-inch shell passed straight through the roof of the dugout and failed to explode.

In an attempt to save the three batmen, Private Arthur Whitbread rushed to the spot and regardless of the shells which were falling all around, started to dig them out, scraping the earth away with his hands until joined by Sergeants Gore and Baxter, who came with shovels.'

A letter from 2nd Lieutenant J. Wynham Tomson to Cliff's parents.

'Dear Mr & Mrs Scott,

I am in command of No. 2 Platoon of the 5th Leicestershire Battalion. I have to write that a shell hit the roof of Cliff's dugout. He was unconscious when we took him out but our Medical Officer, Captain Barton, could not possibly have been able to save his life.

He died soon after excavating him. Cliff was one of

the best, always cheery and willing. I would like you to know that his best friends - Privates A. Tovell and T. Robson dug his grave.

I shall miss him very much.

> *Yours sincerely, J. Wyndham Tomson.*
> *2nd Lieutenant. (1/5 Leics).'*

(Private A. Tovell and Private T. Robson have been mentioned earlier).

Clifford wrote a letter to his parents two days before he was killed: *'We got shelled a lot as we were going into the trenches and I had to take cover in a ditch, but I'm all right.'*

A little earlier in the war Clifford was wounded when some shrapnel tore into his thigh, but he recovered after spending two-to-three days at a dressing station. On the 6th September 1915, Lance Corporal A. W. Hanson, who had been a cashier at Wootton Brothers, brought Cliff's personal possessions, plus a few trophies he had picked up, to the family home.

He said of Cliff: *'He was a nice lad, and the affectionate regard shown for him by his officers was shared by all who knew him.'*

Memorial to Captain Frederic Scott M.C. at Stephenson's College.

The Coalville Times of the 10th September 1915 reveals the tragic end of the popular young man who was well known from his time as a telegram messenger. The bravery of Private Arthur Whitbread must not be forgotten. He was a Loughborough man and he battled in vain to save Cliff's life. He sadly lost his own life at St. Elie Left Sector on 28th July 1917. His name can be read on Loughborough's Carillon Memorial.

Many thanks to Barrie and June Scott. Barrie is the son of Robert Scott, who was half-brother to Clifford.

John Summers and Sidney Summers

John Summers.

The brothers John and Sidney Summers were born on Hugglescote's Ashburton Road, the family living at house number 152. Both were born in the 1890s and worshipped at St. John The Baptist Church and also attended the Church School.

John enlisted at Coalville in the first week of the war into the 5th Leicestershire Battalion. At some future date he was switched to the 51st Machine-Gun Corps and promoted to Lance Corporal (2487-53654). After serving over three years on the Western Front John was killed on the 20th July 1918.

Sidney Summers.

His brother Sidney enlisted in early September 1914, also into the 5th Battalion. Although a relatively late entrant it was regimental policy to keep brothers together where possible at this stage of the war. When a good friend of his, Bill Massey, was killed in August 1915, he wrote a very compassionate letter to Bill's parents, explaining how he was killed, and how much he was liked. Sid (3001-240897) remained with the Battalion for three-and-a half years until he was killed on the 24th September 1918 during the storming of the village of Pontruet (St. Quentin Sector), France. The conflict was initially fought in semi-darkness with a thick mist, a heavy barrage and with lots of smoke. This was where Lieutenant Barrett almost lost his life but won the Victoria Cross for leading a charge against an enemy trench bristling with machine-gun posts.

The Battalion lost 4 officers with 7 wounded, and 43 other ranks were lost with 100 wounded. My grandfather fought in this battle and he was of the opinion that there were many cases of self-sacrifice and heroism.

The Battalion sent a letter to Mrs Summers, so perhaps the father had died. If so, the poor lady had lost a husband and two sons.

The Summer's family home was demolished and a house built in the Thirties is sited there.

John and Sid have their names etched on the Coalville Clock Tower Memorial and also on a tablet in St. John The Baptist Church at Hugglescote.

George William Underwood

George was born in Loughborough in 1896 and family circumstances meant that Mr & Mrs. J. Orton of 16, Leicester Road, Whitwick took him into their family as a foster child. They worshipped at Whitwick Parish Church. George enlisted at Coalville into the 5th Leicestershire Battalion ('C' Company), and was a drummer with the battalion band.

He suffered and survived for four years on the Western Front until he too was killed on the 24th September 1918. George (2456-240576) was killed in the storming of the village of Pontruet, which I have previously mentioned. I find it disturbing that another of the Fifty, after serving for so long was killed six weeks before the Armistice. He was twenty-two years of age. He lies buried close to his friend, Cecil Hurley, at Bellingcourt British Cemetery.

George's name can be read on Whitwick Parish Church Memorial and also on the Coalville Clock Tower Memorial.

Lawrence and Thomas Handley Usherwood

These were two of the four sons of Mr & Mrs T. Usherwood of Highfield Street, Coalville. Their father was an engine driver with the local railways.

Lawrence was educated at the Wesleyan School on Belvoir Road, and before the war he worked for Stableford's Wagon Works.

Thomas, born in 1894 was educated at the same school, and was both a Sunday school teacher and a 'preacher on trial'. He was employed on the office staff with Wootton Brothers.

Lawrence Usherwood.

Thomas Usherwood.

They both enlisted in Coalville in early September 1914 and featured in the same Company as Sergeant Major Roland Hill, 5th Leicestershire Battalion.

Roland Hill of 301, Ashby Road, Coalville West was quite a character. He too worked for Stableford's Wagon Works before the war. He knew many of the First Fifty, and did all he could to help and advise them. Early on he wrote in the local Times to inform readers *'that all of my men are in wonderfully good spirits.'* He was wounded slightly on one occasion, and on another (November 1916) was admitted to hospital with 'trench fever'. Before the war he had served eighteen years with the Leicestershire Volunteers and Territorial Army, and had suffered from enteric fever whilst fighting in the South African War. The brave soldier was to receive the Distinguished Conduct Medal before the end of the Great War.

Tom (240587) wrote a letter on the 19th April 1915: *'We have been in action for the first time in the frontline, and you cannot imagine what it is like. It's bullets above, around and everywhere and the large guns fairly deafen you. We are in the thick of the fighting and every man is intent on victory. We have to rough it in many ways, and we are always facing death but we are in good spirits and we are often whistling or singing our favourite songs.*

The Germans are good shots, but our boys are equal to them. Believe me I don't know what the country would have done without the Territorials, and out here there are lots of local men, and we have many a good chat with them. Thank you for sending the Coalville Times, it is so nice and cheery to read home news. We all hope the war will soon be over so that we can return home, but believe me we will not all come back, but I have good faith that I shall come through all right. I read about the Coalville Cup Final, I was in the trenches when it took place. It was the first one I've missed! I hope Whitwick pull it off in the replay. Remember me to all back home, and Lawrence wishes to be remembered.' (Whitwick lost the replay).

Tom also wrote home to tell of his experiences during the Battle of the Hohenzollern on the 13th October 1915:

'We left the billets at 2.30 pm on October 12th in fighting order, knowing what we were going into. The band played us out of the French village and off we went with light hearts determined to do well. We halted at 6.00 pm and had a couple of hours rest and off we went arriving in the trenches at 7.00 am on October 13th. Then we had a bit of a sleep best we could until daylight. The day dawned rather dull and cold, but as the anxious hours passed the sun broke through the clouds and improved our spirits. All at once the great guns broke forth, and our artillery bellowed forth their shells and caused havoc and destruction wherever they fell. You talk about thunderclouds breaking it is not in it! The German trenches were being battered to nothing and the very earth seemed to be shaking under our feet but no one said a word. For an hour or two this went on then the time for the charge began to draw nearer. Hearts were beating and thoughts wandering and I guess many prayers were being muttered.

In our minds we could see our loved ones and our homes - six minutes, five, four, three, two, 'Charge Boys.' Over the parapet we went, officers and men together. Bayonets glistened in the sun and bombs were flying in all directions, and shells were tearing the earth up. But on we Terrier boys went in ranks of open formation. We reached the first German Line and captured it. There was little time for thinking and we breached the second line and cries go up for mercy from them. A struggle then ensues for a redoubt filled with machine-guns and we have Lincolnshires, Tigers, Nottinghamshire and Derby troops with us. Our blood is up and we take the redoubt and we meant to. We advance again but the enemy artillery fire is hellish, words cannot express what it is like. The very earth seems to be going from under our feet. Night came and we held our trenches - to our credit. Thus the Terrier boys have gained a bit more back from the hated Huns. But the sight of it, I cannot tell you words cannot express it. In the night everything is being done, and the wounded are being helped as quickly as possible. Men are out in the open risking their lives carrying our lads back to our trenches. As for myself I was doing the same. My own officer, a braver man has never lived was leading us out when he was hit.

Two of us carried him to safety and bound him up but the poor fellow died within minutes. The last words he said were: 'I have done my best.' And so the rescue work went on, and the rest were digging for their lives to get under cover. All night long it raged. Next day dawned and we had made our position secure and we held it until we were relieved. We marched back to our billets absolutely exhausted and we did justice to a good meal. There were lots of deeds of heroism and I will tell you them one day, we are just so thankful that God has spared us.

Thank you for the Coalville Times, I am always pleased to receive it. Must close now. Remember me to all. Lawrence wishes to be remembered to everyone. We hope you are all quite well. Love, Tom.'

Thomas accidentally shot himself and died from wounds on 22nd March 1917. A Lieutenant H. S. Simpkin wrote to his bereaved parents, *'It is with deepest sympathy that I have to write to inform you of the death of your son. His death occurred under the most unfortunate of circumstances whilst cleaning a revolver. No one was actually with him at the time of the accident and so it is impossible to give you fuller*

details. To me he was more than a friend and I cannot express my feeling at such a happening. May God help you to bear this terrible loss. I have all of his belongings and I will either send them or bring them to you. I am expecting to be home in a very short time and I will make it my duty to call and visit you in Coalville. Again please accept my deepest sympathy.'

The Coalville Times of the 13th April 1917 reports on: 'Coalville Soldiers Sad Death.'

Thomas was 22 years of age when he died, and it was not a self-inflicted wound in the negative sense. Lieutenant Simpkin survived the war.

Lawrence (2698) was promoted to a non commissioned officer and survived the war, along with his other brothers.

The Coalville Times on the 2nd November 1917, recorded that a third brother, J. Usherwood of the Northumberland Fusiliers had been wounded.

Tom was a very clever young man and an excellent writer. His name can be read on the war memorial in the Wesleyan Methodist Church (as can others of the Fifty: namely Cecil Bradshaw, Frederick Hart, James Hall) and on the Coalville Clock Tower Memorial.

Arthur Walker

Arthur was born in 1895 at Coalville. He had a younger brother by the name of Percy and they lived with their parents at 35, James Street in the town. Both brothers were educated at the Wesleyan School on Belvoir Road. Following his education Arthur was employed as a miner at South Leicestershire Colliery. Arthur (2475-240586) enlisted at Coalville in the first week of the war into the 5th Leicestershire Battalion. Unfortunately, little is known of his military career, and

if wounded there are no reports as such. He remained a dutiful soldier with the same battalion throughout the war, completing it as a private soldier, so readers will know just what he experienced. A true survivor.

His brother was a Gunner (13419) in the R.M.A. on H.M.S. 'Temeraire'. He too survived.

As far as can be traced neither were related to Henry Walker (below).

Henry Walker

 Always referred to as Harry. He was born in August of 1895 at Ravenstone to Mr & Mrs George Walker. His father worked for the Coalville Urban District Council on the Kelham Bridge sewerage farm, and the family lived on the Main Street. After leaving school Harry became a miner at the South

Leicestershire Colliery at Ellistown. He was a chorister at the local church and was also a Sunday school scholar. Harry (2479) enlisted at Coalville in the first week of the war, joining the Usherwood brothers in Sergeant Major Roland Hill's Company of the 5th Leicestershire Battalion.

It was in the early hours of the 2nd July 1915 that Harry narrowly avoided death in the infamous Trench

50, near to Hill 60 in the lethal Ypres Salient. A whizz-bang landed and only the zigzag nature of the trench had saved his life. It was a shock nevertheless. The Germans were able to keep their Batteries a mere 220 metres (180 yards) behind their frontline, and pinpointed some area of the Battalion frontline to be hit every three hours. Because the batteries were so close the men heard the 'bang' before the 'whizz', so there was little opportunity of escape.

A few hours afterwards, nineteen-year-old Harry lost his life. It was early morning and, as always, even in this perilous area, the birds were in chorus, when the sudden crack of a rifle silenced them for a few minutes. Harry, on guard duty had raised his head a little too far and he slumped to the bottom of the trench. Friends rushed to help him but it was evident that he had died within seconds.

A close friend, and one of the First Fifty, Private Arthur Congrave wrote a letter to his father, Thomas Congrave on the 2nd July 1915. He informed him that Harry had been killed, sniped at 6.00 am and that he died almost straightaway, thus suffering no pain. He also said that he would inform Rev. S. Dowling, rector of Ravenstone, and to ask him to convey the sympathy from himself and Private William Kendrick (another soldier from the village) to Mrs Walker.

Harry Walker wrote to his cousin in Ravenstone the day before he died:

'I received your welcome letter. We have not done a lot this last fortnight but they will soon have something in store for us. This is our second day in these trenches and we are getting on fine but we do get shelled a lot. Two of us went out on our hands and knees to see what we could find and ran into a German trench. We did scuttle! One chap let his horse run away the day before we came here, so he came with us and got killed the next day. We have just had a fresh lot to reinforce us. Girls who write letters out here have caused many a chap to get killed. They write asking for this and that and the chaps go out to try and get them and many a one never comes back.

We are about a thousand yards from the Germans now, because we took this trench of them and they had to fall back into a wood.'

Private Harry Walker's name can be read on the War Memorial in Ravenstone Churchyard.

Frederick and John William Williamson

John Williamson.

Frederick was born in 1892 and John (called Jack) William in 1893 to Mr & Mrs William Williamson at Whitwick. The family moved to 68, Park Road, Coalville around the turn of the century. The brothers were regular member of Ebenezer Baptist Sunday School and congregation. Both were miners at Whitwick Colliery, however, Jack had a studious nature and attended evening classes and could write in Pitman's shorthand. (Possibly taught by Walter Baker, one of the First Fifty). He was also studying mining engineering and a bright future had been forecast for the intelligent young man. The two brothers were very well known in the town, as they used to give character-songs at many a concert, and were frequently in demand in northwest Leicestershire.

Both Frederick (2702) and Jack (2693) enlisted in Coalville, in early September and late August 1914 respectively, and served with the 5th Battalion of the Leicestershire Regiment.

On the 23rd April 1915 at Ebenezer Baptist Chapel the Pastor read out both brothers' names in a roll of honour for members who were fighting in the Armed Forces.

Jack was a respected corporal in 'A' Company when he was killed on 24th March 1916.

Jack's last letter home was dated the 17th March 1916:

'We are having a few days rest about nine miles behind the firing line, after being in the trench for six days and nights. It has been the heaviest going since I have been out here, with plenty of fighting and work both day and night. I must tell you both that I am as happy as the day is long.

What may seem strange to you, but it is strongly in my head is that what is to be, will be, and so what is the use of caring. One has only to die the once. The weather is now a lot better than it was, thank goodness. We are only a matter of yards from the German frontline and we have some hot 'dos', what with bombs, shells, bullets and the blowing up of mines. We have recently relieved some French troops, and this will make the British line longer. I can't tell you what I would like you to send me, so it might be as well for you to send me what you like. I am sorry to hear of your illness, Dad, and I hope you get better soon. Give my love to my dear mother, and please remember me to all relatives and friends. Best of love, Jack.'

The Battalion was in trenches on the slopes of Vimy Ridge, and as was usually the case, an enemy barrage had been pounding them.

The War Diary quotes: 'The bombardment of March 23rd left our frontline in a terrible condition, and we decided to build a new line 55 metres (50 Yards) to the rear. In the meantime we had to hold the frontline with just the odd post, and the front parapets also had to be repaired. The night was spent doing this, as best we could, but the following afternoon we were hammered again.'

This time 'A' Company suffered most with Corporal J. Williamson and a Private George Spicer (of Wymeswold) being killed. The trench was blown in for several yards and a dugout completely demolished. Jack was twenty-three years of age.

The letter from one brother explaining how the other died.

On the 25th March 1916, Frederick wrote home to his parents:

'I hardly know where to start this letter. I hope you are all well at home, but I can hardly say I am well, as last night was the worst night that I have known out here. I regret to say that I have very sad news for you this time, and it is making it hard to write. I am sure it will be a big blow to you all. I must not go on a roundabout fashion to tell you. Dad, I regret to say you have lost one of your best sons in this campaign. Our dear Jack passed away peacefully last night. I am sure it will be a great blow to you all, especially my darling mother, but Dad, break the news as quietly as you can.

It has been a great blow to me. I did not know until it was all over, and I just got there in time for one last look at our dear Jack. Oh, Dad, I didn't think I should feel it like this, after what I have got used to. It came as such a shock, and has cut me up completely. It

happened at 3.00 pm, and I didn't know until 9.00 pm. Jack's Company was in the firing line and he was sitting with just three other men when the Germans started sending trench mortars over. They are a big kind of shell and very explosive, and one dropped near to them and buried all four. Jack was the first to be dug out but he was unconscious. The doctor said his ribs were very badly broken and also had head wounds. I was on duty on the telephone when it happened, and so I did not find out until 8.30 pm. A pal, Jack Smith, (who was to die at Pontruet) and I went to the dressing station and I had the surprise of my life - they were just taking him away. Jack will be buried quietly just behind the firing line. I could not go to see him buried, but I will go and see his grave tomorrow. Don't take it too much to heart, Dad, for like so many other comrades he died fighting for his country and doing his duty. Our Jack never flinched from his duty and he was well respected by his men. I am sorry I didn't see him before they put him in his blanket, but perhaps it was as well. They tell me he died peacefully and that he didn't linger long. The doctor said that if he had lived he would have been a cripple. It may be hard for you but always remember your son died a glorious death, and he is one of Britain's heroes. Write to me as soon as you can and tell me how mother takes it. I expect you will hear from the War Office soon. Don't worry over me Dad, I shall trust in the Lord to give me strength to endure this to the end. You know the saying when Christ was on the Cross; 'I go to prepare a place for you". I trust that when the time comes we shall all be ready to meet our Maker, and all be reunited around the blood-washed throne in Heaven, where we shall have neither pain nor sorrow. So, Dad, comfort darling mother.'

2nd Lieutenant G. Russell wrote to Jack's parents on the 25th March 1916:

'I am writing this note with very deep regret. We have lost one of our best NCOs. Yesterday, your son, whilst on duty was killed by the explosion of a 'sausage' shell sent over by a trench mortar. He did not suffer much; he died fifteen minutes after we had dug him out. The doctor said there was no hope, as he was suffering from internal pressure on the brain.

He was very well liked by both his men and his officers. He was always prepared to do his duty, and *more than his duty. I ask you to accept the deepest sympathy of all the officers and men, his friends, in this your terrible loss.*

Yours sincerely, G. Russell (2nd Lieutenant).'

It was reported that just before his death he was made a cadet and informed that he would shortly be sent to an Officer Training Unit.

Jack's name is etched on the Coalville Clock Tower Memorial and also on a tablet in Ebenezer Baptist Chapel.

In June 1917 Frederick wrote to the parents of Sergeant J. Harper, another of the Fifty, explaining how they were like brothers and how he missed Jack (Harper). They had served together for nearly two and a half years at the frontline. Frederick survived the war.

Everard Victor Woolley

Victor was born on the 20th May 1892 at 35, Breach Road at Hugglescote. His father, John Thomas Woolley was a railway guard with the L. and N.W.R. He went to Christ Church School on London Road, Coalville and also the Wesleyan School on Belvoir Road where the headmaster was Thomas Frith. Victor was a fine athlete, and in particular was a keen footballer. On leaving school at the age of fourteen he trained as an engineer at Stableford's Wagon Works.

Victor was a quiet, sensible and intelligent man who always believed that if a job was worth starting then it certainly was worth finishing. He was an excellent dancer, and often took to the stage with such friends as Arthur Newberry Choyce, Cyril Walton and Amos Jarvis. For several years before the war he worshipped at Ebenezer Baptist Chapel.

Shortly before the war he took-up employment at South Leicestershire Colliery at Ellistown.

He enlisted at Coalville in the first week of the war into the 5th Leicestershire Battalion and at that time resided with his sister, Mrs J. Harrison of Breach Cottages, Hugglescote.

The pastor at Ebenezer Chapel read out his name on the 23rd April 1915 as part of a Roll of Honour for men serving with the King's Armed Forces.

Victor (2512) battled through the early stages of the war and was upset when his best pal, Walter Gray, was killed when the Germans detonated a mine under Trench 50 in the Ypres Salient. Long though he tried, he and others had to give up the search for his body. On the 26th July 1915 he wrote a letter to Walter's father explaining what had happened.

Victor gained promotion to the rank of corporal, and on 24th May 1917 showed great bravery and endurance during a tremendous barrage, sufficient to receive the Military Medal. The Battalion was fighting in the area of Lievin, near to Lens in France, and our frontlines were facing Hill 65. As usual this lofty position gave the enemy a huge advantage, which they utilised to great effect, especially with artillery accuracy. The Battalion held Riaumont Hill, and on its summit was an observation post, and naturally this was constantly being shelled: *'For several hours he remained under shell-fire repairing severed telephone wires and re-established the communication which had been broken.'* The Coalville Times proudly published all of this information shortly after the event.

'Military Medal - Number 240591, Corporal E.V. Woolley, Leicestershire Regiment. Awarded the Military Medal at Cite-de-Riaumont, on 24th May 1917, during which time he mended twenty breaks in the line. For over two years in France and Flanders he has done the most excellent work with the signal section. He has always been the first to volunteer for any dangerous work on the line. Recommended for immediate award. (31st May 1917).

The gallant soldier was one of the first Fifty Territorials to leave Coalville in October 1914. Shortly afterwards Victor was wounded. A bullet entered through his left abdominal wall leaving a small hole, and exited by his right rear wall with a jagged effect. He pushed his intestine in and held it until being rescued, it was then strapped-up.'

Victor was very lucky. The bullet missed his kidneys, bladder and liver and he survived. Usually such wounds result in death due to septicaemia caused by an inevitable lack of hygiene in the frontlines.

Thanks to hospital surgeons he recovered and after

The wedding of 2nd Lieutenant E. V. Wooley to Drusilla Adams of Ellistown.

convalescence and home leave returned to his unit. Continued good work resulted in Victor being sent in October 1918 to the Officer Training Unit at St. John's College, Oxford, and also he played football for the cadet team.

In early January 1919 he took leave to marry his fiancée, Drusilla Adams, and a carpet of snow was something of a feature at the wedding. Victor returned to Oxford and was commissioned as a 2nd Lieutenant on the 17th March 1919.

After leaving the army in 1919 the couple lived with his mother at 27, South Street, Ellistown.

He had hoped to become an engineer, however the pay was insufficient to support a wife and shortly a child. He took the best-paid job available and laboured on the coalface at South Leicestershire Colliery. In the evenings he studied at Coalville Technical College, being taught by Mr Haddock on aspects of mining. Victor and Drusilla had three children, Simeon (Sim), Maurice and Betty.

He was promoted to an over-man, then a deputy at Ibstock Colliery, and they were then living at 215, Leicester Road, (known as 'Colliery Row' in Ibstock). Victor was eventually promoted to under-manager at Measham Colliery. He also worked at Ellistown Colliery.

His final home was at 167, Melbourne Road, Ibstock and it was there where he died from a heart attack on the 12th September 1954. He is buried in Hugglescote's Station Road Cemetery. Sim told me: *'When father worked on the coalface he would come home for a bath, and I would help to wash the coal dust from his back. His back was pitted with shrapnel, and often it would come to the surface and I would pick it out from under blisters.*

His bullet wound would often weep, and dirt would stick to it and it looked just like a tattoo.'

Daughter Betty told me the very moving story: *'My father was in his sixties, and it was a terrible winter's evening and as usual he was on his bicycle heading for home. It was dark and the rain was pelting down. By chance, my husband and I were in our car driving along Whitehill Road in Ellistown. I looked out and saw my poor father on his bicycle, cap on his head and peddling away in his normal determined manner (About twenty minutes by bike). At that moment I realised just what a hard life their generation had suffered and endured.'*

Sim was an outstandingly good local boxer, and fought bravely during W.W.2 in the Navy.

Many thanks to Simeon (now deceased) and his wife Margaret.

On the photograph of the First Fifty, the officer sitting immediately behind the dog is Captain (Jack) John Puxley White Jamie of 99, Belvoir Road, Coalville. He remained with the 5th Battalion throughout the conflict, rising to the rank of colonel after the war, and later became a General Practitioner in Coalville. His house, now demolished, was known as 'Scotlands' on the Forest Road. He moved to Glen Parva, a village southeast of Leicester. I was informed he lived from 1892-1954. His brother, Captain Robert Cuthbert Scott Jamie of the same address was in the Royal Flying Corps. The officer on the right is Lieutenant Roland Farmer of Ashby de la Zouch, later Captain in command of 'C' Company, who was killed at Vimy Ridge on the 22nd March 1916. The third man may well be Sergeant Stone.

THE FAMOUS FIFTY
of the
ROYAL LEICESTERSHIRE REGIMENT

They proudly pocketed the 'King's-shilling' in August 1914 at the outbreak of war.
Patriotic young men joining 'The Tigers' in strength, add ten to a double score.
Moulded from northwest Leicestershire clay with a resilient gritty seam,
And they were tough, strong and prepared to smash the Prussian expansion dream.

Khaki-clad and taught basics whilst camped on High Tor, a Charnwood Forest floor.
Came one frosty October dawn and a call to pack up and join a battalion corps.
A service at Hugglescote Church and a street march to Coalville railway station,
With a beat of the drums, a merry tin whistle and thousands cheered in heroic ovation.

Billets at Luton and Sawbridgeworth and manoeuvres intensified the training.
Hence a military unit, forgotten thoughts of farm-work, railroads and mining.
In February 1915 they cross-Channelled to Le Havre, near to the battle-zone,
Where 'a contemptible little army' buried many a comrade, now poppies overgrown.

Leicestershire 5th Battalion on the Western Front in the trenches of Flanders and France.
Parlez vous at Armentieres, and poppy petals fell as Ypres took a defensive stance.
The summer of 1915 became life's winter for young men buried at Sanctuary Wood,
And October rains washed away the gas and blood at Hohenzollern, but not for good.

Snowy Vimy Ridge of early 1916 saw trench mines and sniping for our suffering band.
Ten days to refit at Lucheux with spring sunshine and dappled shade from woodland.
July 1st, the opening day of the Somme when Picardy roses bloomed at dawn,
And withered in the battle heat of machine-guns to fall in fields of corn.

1917, a return to familiar Loos and Lens with its coalfields and war-scarred history.
Very few of the 'famous fifty' remained, 'twas futile to predict anyone's destiny.
1918, a famous victory, breaching the fortifications on the Hindenberg Line,
As Armistice Day declared war's end, may the memory of the fifty forever shine.

Twenty-two of the fifty returned to their Leicestershire homes after four war-years.
Fifty years on a veteran held a photograph and peered at familiar old faces through tears.
It was a frosty October morning in 1914 and taken in front of his fiancée's home,
And now only a few are left, the other survivors buried in a gritty, clay loam.

Michael Kendrick.
15th September 2003

The Clock Tower Memorial

The official programme of events classifies the above as: *'The Coalville Urban Area War Memorial, and it was unveiled by Mrs. Booth of Gracedieu Manor at 2.30 pm on Saturday, 31st October 1925.'*

The Coalville Times of the 6th November 1925 reports: *'Fully ten thousand people, representing practically half the entire population of the urban district, assembled at the Memorial Square to pay their respects to the 354 men from this locality who gave their lives in the Great War. Few towns can boast such a splendid monument to the gallant men who responded so well in their country's hour of need. Never has the town ever witnessed a public ceremony that was more reverent or dignified.'*

form continuous panels terminating at the clock dials, around which are carved laurel wreathes of stone. The summit of the Tower is faced with stone, having panelled concave sides, with a bold stone coping as finish. The Tower is equipped with an electric clock having a five feet dial on each side, and fitted with a striking gear for striking the hours upon a bell, which is fixed on the outside of the flat roof of the Tower.'

Order of Proceedings. The Coalville Company of the 5th Leicestershire Battalion, under the Command of Captain Jamie, assembled at 1.30 pm in Marlborough Square. Headed by the Regimental Band they marched to their position in Memorial Square.

The programme contains information regarding the Memorial. *'It is 13 feet 6 inches square at its base, rising to a total height of 68 feet above pavement level. The base has approach steps on the north, south, east and west sides, supported by wing-walls in local rubble granite, leading to a landing surrounding the Tower. The lower part of the Tower is specially designed to accommodate the name tablets, which are executed in Cornish granite, and upon which are inscribed the names of the Fallen in lead letters. The main shaft of the Memorial is faced with Staffordshire multi-coloured bricks in cement, and the lines of the name tablets are carried up the main shaft to*

At the same time a procession of ex-servicemen and a detachment of 'C' squadron of the Leicestershire Yeomanry marched from the Market Place at Whitwick to Memorial Square.

At 1.50 pm a procession of ex-servicemen left Forest Road corner, Hugglescote, headed by the surviving members of the '**First Fifty**' and marched with the Hugglescote and Ellistown Band to Memorial Square. They were following the route of the First Fifty back in October 1914*

At 2.00 pm a procession of ex-servicemen marched from the end of London Road, headed by the

Photographs taken from the Coalville Times newspaper covering the unveiling of the Clock Tower.

Hugglescote Town Band, marched to Memorial Square.

At 2.25 pm the procession assembled in Memorial Square. At 2.30 pm the congregation sang: 'O God, our help in ages past'. There followed the unveiling ceremony, the 'Last Post' and one-minutes silence. After Reveille came prayers and then the Very Reverend Canon Walters dedicated the Tower 'to the glory of God, and in memory of our Brothers who were faithful unto death'.

Lieutenant Colonel R. E. Martin C.M.G. who served with the 5th and 4th Leicestershire Battalions gave a short address, in which he said:

'At this time Coalville's citizens will have on their minds, certainly as I have as an old 5th Battalion man, those First Fifty men who volunteered to make up the 5th Battalion strength. They trained at Thringstone Institute, joined the Battalion at Luton, and went over the Channel in February of 1915.'

After prayers the Regimental Band played 'Land of Hope and Glory.'

The placing of wreaths followed a final hymn, 'Now thank we all our God.' The first wreath was placed by the organising committee, represented by Mr. B. Drewett, Mr. J. Bennett, Mr. T. Hatter and Mr. T. McCarthy, all who lost dear ones in the war. There followed the laying of a wreath from the Urban Council, which was described as an act of homage from 20,000 fellow townsmen.

The Coalville Times of the 6th November 1925 describes one of the earliest wreaths. *'A magnificent floral tribute from the First Fifty. From a bed of beautiful white flowers stood out twenty-two red roses. (Only twenty-two of the Fifty came back). The inscription on the card reads: 'a token of remembrance to our pals in Flanders", and heads in the congregation were bowed.'*

Wreaths were placed from many employers who lost men including Messrs Stableford's and Wootton Brothers. Hundreds were placed; the crowd remained very silent and sympathetic. Four men of the 5th Battalion, one on each corner of the base of the Memorial, stood with bowed heads, leaning on reversed rifles. The finale was 'God save the King', and thus closed an eventful and memorable day. The Tower was electrically illuminated in the evening and was visited by hundreds of visitors the following day.

The article does not mention who placed the wreath from the Fifty, but it is my hope that it was Captain Jabez Emmerson. D.C.M. He enlisted as a rank and file soldier, and by his leadership and bravery rose to command a Company. The die was cast, and from that moment on the First Fifty became known as the 'Famous Fifty' as a result of the town's appreciation of just what they had achieved. The majority of the ten thousand congregation who witnessed the above have now departed, and it is my hope that this book will keep the flame of memory burning for a good few generations to come.

Author's Comment

The Famous Fifty were undoubtedly the very earliest of civilian volunteers to serve in what was to become known as trench warfare. These trench-systems enforced a static-style of warfare that was an entirely new phenomenon, and henceforth the casualties were proportionately extremely high considering the majority of the heavy fighting was confined to a relatively small area of battle. I have studied many books on the Great War, and I find it unfair to squarely lay the blame on any particular section of the military or political field. I believe it was a combination of imperialist and political circumstances, together with the development of massively destructive weapons, notably artillery guns and the savage thirst of the machine-gun. The onus was always on the Allies to attack and force the Central Powers from the territory they had occupied. The enemy were quite prepared to construct huge defensive redoubts, and entice their opponents to attack and suffer the consequences.

You now know that twenty-eight of the Famous Fifty died during the conflict, a good many in 1915 when they were in their late teens or early twenties. As for the survivors, most suffered physically and mentally for the remainder of their lives. How did they endure such a catastrophic physical and chemical attack on their bodies and minds for four years? They were not professional soldiers in August 1914, not even territorial soldiers and only qualified after a three-month crash course.

In the winter and early spring of 1915 these youngsters were pitched against well-trained professionally minded enemy troops, and from June 1915 they battled for nearly four months in the 'Salient of Death', Ypres. Surviving member of the First Fifty, in one form or another, endured as much pain and suffering as any soldier in the Great War, invariably many times more so! Afterwards, on returning home they were expected to immediately step-back into their civilian occupations, and commence once again on the treadmill of life. There was no counselling, and for the lads who were permanently injured such pensions were cruel and contemptuous. There was no compensation culture and little sympathy, because the majority of the civil population had little, if any understanding of those new horrors of war.

Also consider that when soldiers returned, they found many colleagues involved in war-production had received promotions and were financially secure. The survivors found consolation within themselves at Toc-H, ex-Servicemen Clubs and the Royal British Legion. Great Britain in 1919 was not 'a land fit for heroes.' The old soldiers sat in public houses, sometimes drank too much to forget or to loosen their tongues and discuss shared horrors, nightmares, often shedding tears. Today's counsellors recommend such discussions but our heroes were looked down upon as boozers and 'good for nothings'. If they needed a couple of days off from work due to an old war wound, tongues would wag and they were called 'skivers'. After the appalling influenza epidemic of 1919 there followed the 1926 Miners' Strike. Generally speaking wages were poor, there was insufficient food, housing was very basic, overcrowded and unsanitary, and infant death rates were rising. Who was to blame? Our country was rendered virtually bankrupt by the upheavals of the war, and the same applied to the rest of Europe. The Great War generation was a victim to imperialist and political greed, military developments, and the old adage: time and consequence, it was just waiting to happen. Alphabetically Victor Woolley was the last of the Fifty, yet to my mind he epitomised the dreadful pity and tragedy that broke the heart of a generation. Poets describe my feeling so accurately: *The Lost Flower of a Generation.'* They started with little; suffered throughout their lives from the consequences of four years of hell. There was no escaping their nightmares, and had to work like slaves to support families through desperately fraught times.

Their reward? Very little and soon they saw their sons die in the skies or on the battlefields of World War Two.

Upon retirement, those that made it, more often than not were dead within a few years, but in common with the finest values of mankind took nothing with them. I repeat, and with no apology for doing so, the survivors of the First Fifty suffered as much and more than most during the Great War!

To my mind all were heroes, and the Famous First Fifty had two other details in common. Firstly, they all lived in North West Leicestershire, and secondly they were all members of the 'Tigers,' the Royal

Leicestershire Regiment. I sincerely hope my book will go some way towards ensuring that the above names, indeed all of the names listed in this book will be remembered. I hope that present and future societies will appreciate the huge debt that is owed to them. We owe them our freedom, our present day high standard of living, and finally our very lives.

I dearly hope that young folk will read my book, and having done so, will appreciate what war memorials and the names etched upon them represent.

'Once, they too were young.'

Michael Kendrick.

The First Fifty, 1914.
Front row: Numbered from left: No.8 Bill Massey, No. 9 Fred Briers.
Second row: No.1 Edgar Boot, No.2 Charles Hatter, No.3 Walter Baker, No.4 George Bennett, No. 6 Captain J Jamie, No. 7 Lt. R Farmer, No.9 Charles Cavendish.
Third row: No.1 Cecil Beadman, No.9 Dennis Hodgetts, No.10 William Emmerson, No.11 Jabez Emmerson.
Back row: No.1 Thomas Catlow, No.2 Arthur Congrave, No.7 Victor Wooley, No.9 Walter Handford.

The terraced homes of No. 2, William Baker and No.4, Wilfred Robinson, Ashburton Road, Hugglescote, were replaced in the nineteen thirties by the above detatched property.

Edgar Boot lived at 43 Park Road, Coalville.

Cecil Bradshaw crossed the step at 5 Gutteridge Street, Coalville and never returned.

Fred Briers and his wife, Nellie, married in the nineteen twenties and spent all of their married life at 186 Ashburton Road, Hugglescote. They had three children, Mary, Ted and Pat.

Bill Cowley departed his home at 118 Central Road, Hugglescote only to be entombed by a mine-blast on Vimy Ridge in France.

Walter Gray was living with his Auntie at 183 Belvoir Road, Coalville. His body was never found after a mine detonation in Trench 50 at Ypres in Belgium, 1915.

Walter Handford lived at 95 Highfield Street, Coalville before the Great War.

The happy-go-lucky Frederick Hart's home, 35 London Road, Coalville is now an accountant's office. I think he would have been amused by such an event.

Charles Hatter was born at 13 Forest Road, Hugglescote and lived there until 1914.

John and Sidney Summers lived with their parents at 152 Ashburton Road, Hugglescote before the Great War. Their terraced home was replaced in the nineteen thirties by this property. Both brothers were killed in 1918 in separate incidents.

Arthur Walker lived at 35 James Street, Coalville.

Frederick and John Williamson lived at 68 Park Road, Coalville in 1914. Frederick survived the war, however John was killed by a trench mortar at Vimy Ridge in March 1916.

Pre-war home of Walter Baker, 20 Park Road, Coalville.

Arthur Congrave lived in 29 Wash Lane, Ravenstone. His leg was amputated during the war.

James Hall never returned to his home at 86 Belvoir Road, Hugglescote.

175 Central Road, Hugglescote, the home of William Newbold. He died in 1917. Next door lived Arthur Newbury Choyce, an officer in the same batallion and a Great War poet.

Captain Jabez Emmerson D.C.M. lived at 157 Broomleys Road, Coalville from the nineteen-thirties until his death in 1980. He was the last to die.

John Harper's home. He was killed soon after a spell of leave at this house.

John Lowe lived in 'Albion Cottages', built 1891, 35 Oxford Street, Coalville.

Dennis Hodgetts with daughter Jean in 1932 at 234 Ashby Road, Coalville.

The Hodgetts old home. The same house in 2004.

Shortly after the Great War, Walter Handford opened a little greengrocer shop at 121 Belvoir Street, Coalville. It now stands empty after forty odd years of being T Frith, Family Butchers.

Coalville's first memorial to the Great War dead. The memorial was built into the wall of the railway station and was soon replaced by the Clock Tower memorial.

The Clock Tower Memorial, floodlit in November 1945.

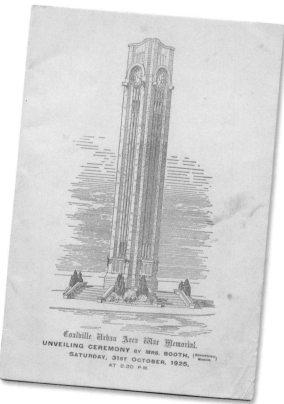

A booklet invitation to the unveiling ceremony.

Christ Church, London Road, Coalville. A view from the rear of the church. Four of the Fifty worshipped here, all returned safely.

Ebenezer Chapel where seven of the Fifty worshipped. Two were to die in battle.

On the 23rd April 1915, the Pastor read out to a packed Chapel a Roll of Honour bearing the names of 39 scholars serving with the Kings Forces.

Gwen and Denis Baker, son of Walter Baker, one of the Fifty, outside Ebenezer.

Ebenezer Chapel Memorial Tablet.

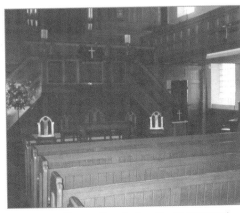

The interior of Ebenezer Chapel, where Charles Hatter wed Hetty Palmer on the 4th November 1918.

S 8691   COUNCIL SCHOOLS, COALVILLE.

Bridge Road
School, Coalville.

Bridge Road School's first
Christmas. Many boys died as
young men during W.W.1.

Wesleyan Chapel,
Belvoir Road,
Coalville.

Baptist Chapel,
London Road,
Coalville.

Ravenstone's Church Memorial including the names of
Harry Walker, George Andrews and Harry Congrave.

CHURCH & LYCH GATE, HUGGLESCOTE.

PROPOSED NEW CHURCH HUGGLESCOTE

St. John The Baptist Church, Hugglescote, where fifteen of the Fifty worshipped. Twelve were killed in action.

Illustration for the proposed St. John The Baptist Church

Menin Gate Memorial, Ypres, showing the name of Bill Massey.

St. John The Baptist Memorial Tablet with ninety eight names.

'Great battles were won on the playing fields of Eton College.' I feel very proud to write that on St. John The Baptist Church School's old playground, thirteen young boys had a merry time until as young men, they progressed to the battlefields of France and Flanders. Nine failed to return and their names can be read on the Church's Memorial Tablet. (W. Pettitt was a pupil and later moved to Ellistown).

On the 19th March 1915, the headmaster of the school anounced a Roll of Honour with the names of sixty three ex-boys serving in the King's Forces.

The grave of Charles and Hetty Hatter.

AT THE GOING DOWN OF THE SUN

It is a very sad issue to find that the above Memorial Tablets, for so many years gracing London Road Baptist Chapel in Coalville, are surplus to requirements after the Chapel moved to nearby Charnborough Road. I hope the readers of this book will say a prayer for the souls of the thirty young men who laid down their lives for our future, only to be forgotten by their chapel in less than a century after their deaths!

A. Wesson. Sherwood Foresters. 8/3/15

John Manders. 2nd Leicestershire Battalion. 15/3/15

Samuel Boot. 5th Leicestershire Battalion. 15/4/15
One of the Famous Fifty

Thomas Dooley. 2nd Leicestershire Battalion. 1/5/15

C. H. Wesson. Sherwood Foresters. 9/5/15

Charlie Jewsbury. 5th Leicestershire. 6/6/15

Frank Martin. 1st Leicestershire. 11/6/15

Clifford Scott. 5th Leicestershire. 1/9/15
One of the Famous Fifty

Sten Hardy. 2nd Leicestershire. 13/1/16

H. Geary. On loose stone

Thomas Black. 5th Leicestershire. 5/10/16

H. G. Wharmby

J. H. Mawer. Royal Sussex Regiment. 16/10/16

A. S. Heward

F. E. Tyler. Manchester Battalion. 31/7/17

A . Martin. 17/8/17

Clarkson C. Woodcock. 1st Leicestershire Battalion 20/11/17

E. Amos. Royal Warwickshire. 3/12/17

Victor Hancox. 2/5th Leicestershire Battalion 6/12/17

L. A. P. Finch. R. F. A. 21/3/18

P. Horn

Frederic Scott. 9th Leicestershire Battalion. 27/5/18

Samuel Beck. 5th Leicestershire. 11/5/18

J. F. Colver. East Yorkshire Regiment. 10/10/18

W. A. Berrisford. Royal Air Force. 7/10/18

Percy Cliff. 2/5th Leicestershire Battalion. 11/10/18

A. Ford.

W. H. Hordern.

T. M. Hordern

J. A. Jeffcoat

INDEX

Part One

First Fifty Soldiers

Andrews G., Pte. 28

Bennett J.G., Pte. 26, 28

Emmerson J., Cpl. .28

Gray W., Pte. 28

Hart F. W., Pte. 8

Hatter C., Pte. .5, 26

Massey W., Pte. 28

Scott C., Pte. 28

Walker H., Pte. 28

First Fifty casualties 11, 12, 13,15, 19, 22, 24,
. . . . .26, 27, 28, 30

Officers

Aked G., Lt. 11

Banwell G.E., Lt. 20

Barratt J.C., Lt. V.C. 19, 23

Barton M.H., Capt .29

Choyce A.N., 2 Lt .17

Faire R.A., Capt. 29

Farmer, R., Lt. .15, 94

Hamilton I. Sir, General 7

Hastings P.C., Capt. 29

Hills J.D., Capt 27

Jackson W., Capt. 16, 32

Jamie, J. P. W., Capt. 94
Jones C.H., Lt. Col. 12
Langdale E.G., Capt. 29
Martin R.E., Capt. 29
Milne J., Capt. 24
Moore A., Capt 4, 12, 18, 20, 22, 26
Moss H.J., Lt. 29
Shields C., Capt. 21
Toller W.S., Major 14, 30

Other ranks
Barney W., L.Cpl. 26
Burton A., Pte. 21
Cato H., Pte 30
Clayson, L.Cpl. 29
Cross L., Pte. 30
Hill J.R., Sgt. Major 16, 32
Lester T., Cpl. 20
Stone, Sgt. 7
Ward O., Pte. 29, 30
Woolhouse F., Pte. 30

Mining operations 12, 13, 26, 27, 28, 56, 57

Battlefield locations
Bart's Alley 29
Big Willie 29
Bomb Corner 13, 26
Cambrin Right 21, 22
Double Crassier 19
Forgan's Trench .23, 76
Fosse 3 . . . . .19, 20, 75
Fosse 8 . . . . .21, 29, 30, 75
Gommecourt 16, 18, 19, 20, 32
Hill 50 . . . . .24, 26
Hill 60 . . . . .12, 13, 26
Hill 65 . . . . .19, 20
Hindenburg Line 23, 24, 76
Hill 70 12
Hohenzollern Redoubt 14, 21, 29-31
La Bassee Canal .22, 54
Lake Dug-outs 13
Little Willie 29
Lorette Ridge 19
Mad Point 29, 30
Madagascar Cottages 29
Maple Copse 26, 74
Marqueffles farm 19
Pigeon Wood 32

Riqueval Bridge 24
Sanctuary Wood 13, 26, 28, 74
Shrapnel Corner 13
St. Elie 21
Trench Leicester Street 32
Trench Midland 32
Trench 34 26
Trench 35 . . . . .13, 26
Trench 36 . . . . .13, 26
Trench 37 13
Trench 49 13
Trench 50 . . . . .13, 26-28
Trench 51 13
Vimy Ridge 14, 15, 57, 92

Locations - England
Beech Hill School 6
Bishops Stortford 9
Ceylon Hall 6
Coalville Station 7, 8
Coalville East Station 7
Derby Station 6
Duffield 6
Harlow Station 9
High Tor 7
H.M.S. Andania 12
Loughborough Drill Hall 7
Luton 6, 7, 9
Much Hadham 9
Sawbridgeworth 9
Southampton 9
S.S. Atlanta 9
S.S. Duchess of Argyle 9
Ware 9
Wigston Barracks 7

Locations - France and Flanders
Albert 15
Annezin 19
Armentiers 11
Arneke Station 11
Bapaume 16
Bellenglise 23
Berguette Station 14
Bethune 19, 22, 29
Beuvry 21
Bienvillers 18
Bouvigny 19
Chocques Station 23

Cite St. Pierre 19

Essars 22

Foncqevillers 16, 32

Gommecourt 16

Gorre 22

Hardifort 10

Hesdignuel 30

Hooge 26

Hulluch 20

La Bassee 23

Le Bizet 11

Leicester Magazine 6

Le Havre 9, 10

Lens 15, 23, 75

Lucheux 15, 16

Le Quesnoy 22

Lievin 19

Locre 13

Loos 14, 19, 22, 29

Marseilles 14

Messines 11, 12

Millencourt 18

Montauban 16

Mont St. Eloi 15

Monchy au Bois 18

Monchy Breton 20

Neippe Forest 14

Neuville St. Vaaste 14

Pommiers 18

Pontruet 23, 76

Serre 16

Souastre 16, 18

Souchez 14, 19

St Quentin Canal 23

Sucrerie 16

Vermelles 29

Ypres 11, 13, 26, 28

Zillebeke 12, 13, 26

Part Two

Individuals of the First Fifty
(The Dead in **Bold Type**)

Andrews, George L (2555) 34

Baker, Major (2431) 35

Baker, Walter S. 35-37

Baker, William (2554) .38

Bancroft, James (2564) .38

Bartlam, Frederick (2561) 39

Beadman, Cecil T. (2566) 39-40

Bennett, George H. 40-41

Bennett, J. George (2558) 42

Blackham, Harold G. (2553) 43

Boot, Edgar E. 43

Boot, E. Samuel (1620) 44-45

Bradshaw, A. Cecil (2551) 45-46

Briers, Frederick .46-47

Catlow, Thomas L. 47-48

Cavendish, Charles 53-54

Congrave, Arthur .54-55

Cowley, J. William (2560) 55-58

Cramp, Henry 58

Dedman, Charles (2450) 58-59

Emmerson, Jabez (2532) 59-62

Emmerson, William. H 59-62

Glynn, Frances (2527) 63

Gray, Walter (2528) 63-64

Hall, Isaac (2521) 64

Hall, James H. 64-65

Handford, Walter (2518) 65-68

Harper, Isaac (2522) .68

Harper, John. W. (2523) 68-69

Hart, Frederick W. (2535) 69-71

Hatter, Charles (2534) 71-78

Hodgetts, Arthur, W 80-81

Hurley, Cecil (2579) .81

Lowe, John 82

Massey, William (2512) 82-83

Newbold, William (2493) 84

Pettitt, Walter (2488) 84-85

Robinson, Wilfred (2482) 85

Robson, Thomas (2502) 85

Scott, Clifford E. (2488) 86-87

Summers, John (2487) 88

Summers, Sidney (3001) 88

Underwood, George W. (2456) 88

Usherwood, Lawrence (2698) 88-90

Usherwood, Thomas H. 88-90

Walker, Arthur (2475) 90

Walker, Henry (2479) 90-91

Williamson, Frederick (2702) 91-93

Williamson, John W. (2693) 91-93

Woolley, E. Victor (2512) 93-94